# REEDS
# CREW
# HANDBOOK

**REEDS**

LONDON · OXFORD · NEW YORK · NEW DELHI · SYDNEY

REEDS
Bloomsbury Publishing Plc
50 Bedford Square, London, WC1B 3DP, UK
Bloomsbury Publishing Ireland Limited,
29 Earlsfort Terrace, Dublin 2, D02 AY28, Ireland

BLOOMSBURY, REEDS, and the Reeds logo are trademarks of Bloomsbury Publishing Plc

First published in Great Britain 2012
This edition published 2025

A catalogue record for this book is available from the British Library

ISBN: PB: 978-1-3994-2178-2; eBook: 978-1-3994-2175-1; ePDF: 978-1-3994-2176-8

2 4 6 8 10 9 7 5 3 1

Typeset in Myriad Pro by Susan McIntyre
Printed and bound in India by Replika Press Pvt. Ltd.

MIX
Paper | Supporting
responsible forestry
FSC™ C016779

To find out more about our authors and books visit www.bloomsbury.com
and sign up for our newsletters

For product safety related questions contact productsafety@bloomsbury.com

# REEDS
# CREW
# HANDBOOK

**BILL JOHNSON**

# R E E D S
LONDON · OXFORD · NEW YORK · NEW DELHI · SYDNEY

# CONTENTS

**Introduction**   **6**

**Parts of the Yacht**   **8**

Hull and deck
Below deck

**Living on a Yacht**   **10**

Food and cooking
The fresh water supply
The heads (toilet)
Electricity supply
Rubbish
Sleeping on board

**Ropes and Knots**   **17**

Rope names
Coiling a rope
The winch
Cleating off a rope
Knots

**Yacht under Motor**   **35**

The engine control
Starting the engine
Stopping the engine
Steering under engine
Prop walk
Prop wash off the rudder

**Yacht under Sail**   **44**

How sails work
Trimming the sails

Points of sail
Coming up to wind
Bearing away
Tacking
Gybing
Steering under sail
Steering a compass course
Steering close-hauled
Sailing downwind
The preventer

**Handling the Mainsail**   **65**

Hoisting the mainsail
Dropping the mainsail
Reefing the mainsail
Shaking out a reef

**Handling the Headsail**   **74**

The headsail
Roller furling headsail
Unfurling the headsail
Furling the headsail
Reefing and unreefing the
    headsail
Conventional headsails
Hoisting a headsail
Dropping a headsail
How to fold a sail

**Spinnakers and
Cruising Chutes**   **86**

The spinnaker
The cruising chute

**Advanced Sail Trimming and Racing**   92

Sail shape
Mainsail adjustments
Headsail adjustments
Crew weight

**Berthing**   96

Pontoons
Arriving at a pontoon
Leaving a pontoon
Rafting on other boats
Harbour walls

**Mooring**   119

Swinging moorings
Picking up a mooring
Leaving a mooring
Rafting on a mooring
Fore-and-aft moorings

**Anchoring**   128

Anchoring a yacht
Setting the anchor
Lifting the anchor
The dinghy

**On Passage**   136

Crew tasks and watches
Lookout
Taking bearings
Helming

Cooking and housekeeping
Keeping the log
Off-watch

**At the End of the Trip**   141

Typical end-of-trip tasks
On deck tasks
Below deck tasks

**Safety and Emergencies**   144

Safety briefing
Personal safety
Lifejacket
Safety harness
Gas
Fire
Emergency equipment
Emergencies
Man overboard
VHF Mayday message

**Next Steps: Towards Skippering a Yacht**   163

Crewing experience
Theory knowledge
Practical skills
Technical skills

**Glossary**   169

**Index**   175

## Introduction

The idea of this book is to help you to be a more confident member of a yacht's crew.

There are lots of activities on a sailing yacht that need a crew, and being part of this – in however small a way – is fun and rewarding.

The book goes through all the different activities, and explains:

◆ What's going on.
◆ What individual crew members need to do, and when.

You're not expected to know, or do, everything in this book – as a yacht crew you are part of a team. You help each other, and learn from each other. This book will explain what is happening during the various tasks that the crew undertake, as well as providing detailed instructions for individual crew members.

If you've crewed before, you will find the book a useful reference to remind you what happens in various situations. If you haven't been on a yacht before, it will cover the basics such as cooking, sleeping and how the toilet works (the **heads**, in proper nautical terms), so you can start off with a basic understanding of how the yacht works, and what you do.

As a member of the crew, you are a useful part of the team running the yacht. With sea time and experience your knowledge and skills will increase, and you become more confident and useful. Good crew are very welcome on any yacht. You will find that many yacht skippers are keen to find crew to help them, and this means you get more opportunities to go sailing.

As you go on different yachts you will find that some things are done in different ways depending on the situation, the conditions and the skippers' preferences. Generally, there can be many ways to do things, so you need to be a bit flexible if the skipper decides to do something slightly differently to the way you were taught on your first yacht or sailing course, or indeed differently to the way it's described in this book. Just because it's different doesn't necessarily make it wrong.

See how the different approaches work, and take the opportunity (perhaps later, over a cup of tea or in the pub) to discuss the skipper's reasons for doing things in a particular way. This is all part of the learning process.

Good luck and good sailing!

### *Acknowledgements*

I make no claim of originality for any of the information and advice in this book, and am extremely grateful to everyone who has helped gain the knowledge which I now pass on. (That includes some of the students on sailing courses I have run.)

Many thanks to Ash Woods, who took the time to review the manuscript and make some excellent suggestions.

## Hull and deck

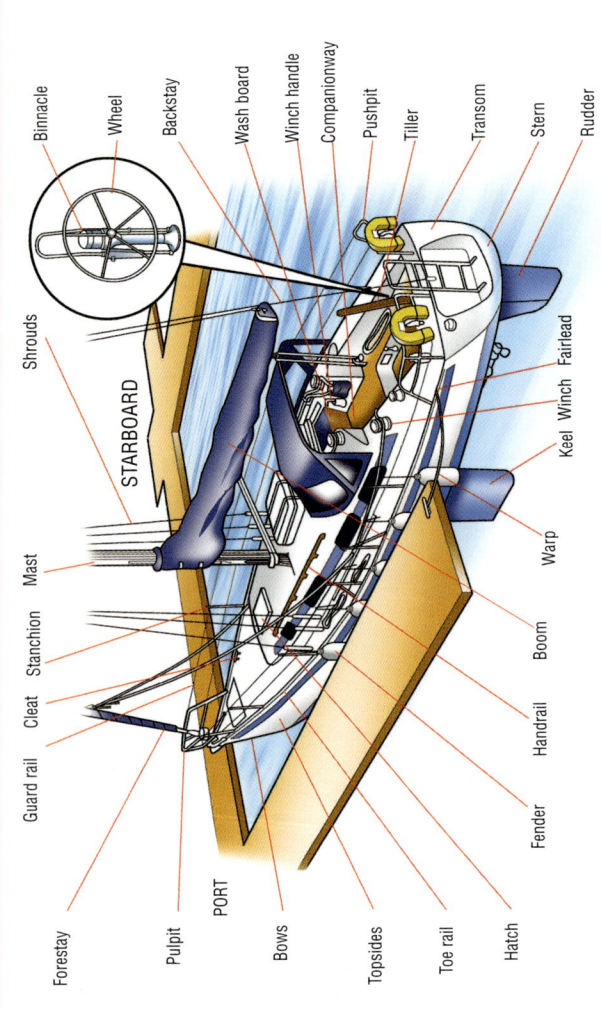

Binnacle
Wheel
Backstay
Wash board
Winch handle
Companionway
Pushpit
Tiller
Transom
Stern
Rudder

Shrouds

STARBOARD

Keel   Winch   Fairlead

Mast

Stanchion

Cleat

Guard rail

Warp

Boom

Handrail

Fender

Forestay

Pulpit

PORT

Bows

Topsides

Toe rail

Hatch

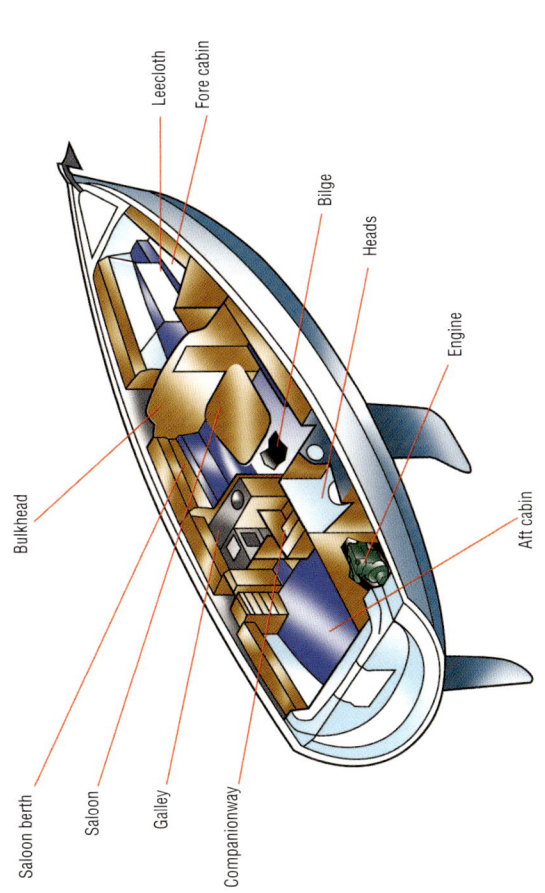

Leecloth

Fore cabin

Bilge

Heads

Engine

Bulkhead

Aft cabin

Saloon berth

Saloon

Galley

Companionway

# Food and water

Yachts have everything you need to live on them, both in a marina and at sea. But things aren't quite the same as living in a house. It helps if you understand the differences and learn to work with them.

## *Food and cooking*

Yachts have limited food storage. Most small yachts have no refrigerator, or if they do they may not run it all the time (see **Electricity supply**, below). So:

◆ Fresh food lasts a limited time, and you need to plan to eat it before it goes off.
◆ Tinned and dried foods (especially rice and pasta) and UHT or powdered milk are useful, because they keep.
◆ Leftovers won't keep for long – eg when tins are opened, they need to be used up.

Anyone who has been camping will be quite familiar with this.

Cooking is generally done on a gimballed cooker in the **galley**, using gas. Gas should be used with care because:

◆ If it leaks or spills, it gathers in the bottom of the boat and can explode (see **Safety and Emergencies**). The skipper will explain the 'routine' for using gas: turn it off at the tap or bottle immediately after use.
◆ There is a limited supply of gas on board, so avoid wastage.

> ✳ **Tip**
> Even with a small gas stove, it is possible to be very creative. Long-distance sailors, for example, often bake fresh bread. You generally try to keep things simple when you are actually at sea, particularly when it's rough. Meals that can be cooked in one pot are very handy.

### *The fresh water supply*

Although you will often have a hot and cold supply in the galley and the heads, the water supply is limited. A typical 35ft yacht may carry about 200 litres of fresh water in the tanks, and this will be needed for drinking, cooking, washing up, washing and cleaning teeth, so it's important to use water carefully.

◆ Never leave a tap running.
◆ Use the plug in the sink, and run as little water as possible.

> ✳ **Tip**
> To brush your teeth, fill a third of a cup or mug with cold water. Use this to wet the brush, rinse your mouth, and swish your toothbrush around in the rest. That's all you need.

◆ The skipper will organise filling the water tanks at the beginning of the trip and whenever you have the opportunity, particularly before a long passage. If you are asked to fill up with water, find the filler cap on the deck (make sure it's the one for water, not fuel!) and use the hose pipes provided onshore.

> ✳ **Tip**
> Run a little water through the hose pipe first – it may have been lying with the end in the sea.

◆ Most marinas and harbours have facilities such as toilets and showers, and it's sensible to use these when you can.

Some large yachts have **reverse osmosis water makers**, but these use a lot of power (see below). Yachts that are at sea for several days may use sea water for activities like washing up. They also carry spare water in containers, for emergencies.

### The heads (toilet)

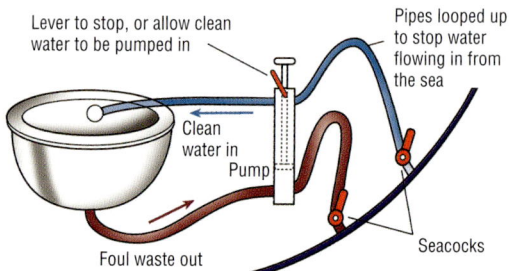

Lever to stop, or allow clean water to be pumped in

Pipes looped up to stop water flowing in from the sea

Clean water in

Pump

Seacocks

Foul waste out

Note: Foul waste is shown going to sea. Sometimes it goes into a holding tank

The heads have a system for flushing sea water through them, so they don't use the fresh water supply.

Some yachts have **holding tanks** for heads waste, which is later pumped out at special shore facilities, or at sea. The heads operate in the same way, whether pumping into a tank or out to sea.

Some harbours don't allow you to use heads that discharge to sea, so you need to use the shore facilities instead.

The skipper should explain how to operate the heads. There are two common systems:

◆ A hand pump with a 'switch' on it:
  ○ Switch one way and the pump simply empties the toilet.
  ○ Switch the other way and clean water is pumped in, at the same time as the toilet is pumped out.

◆ The **Lavac**, which is a vacuum flush system:
  ○ Close the lid, and this seals the top of the toilet.

❍ When you pump out, clean water is automatically sucked in to flush the toilet.
❍ You need to wait for a few seconds after pumping before you can open the lid again – it is held closed by the vacuum.

### What to do, and what NOT to do

◆ There is quite a long pipe from the heads to the outlet, so it is a good idea to flush quite a lot of water through to clear it.
◆ It's a good idea not to leave the heads too full of water (particulary when it's rough). With a Lavac, pump out excess water with the lid open. With the other type, leave the inlet valve closed and pump out excess water.
◆ Ordinary toilet paper actually disintegrates in water, and so it *can* be flushed through the heads.
◆ Other paper *does not disintegrate when wet*, and so *cannot be flushed*. Examples are:
❍ Tissues (like Kleenex)
❍ Kitchen towel
❍ Wet wipes
❍ Sanitary items, cotton wool pads, facial wipes or any other material which you might flush at home.
If these items are flushed, they *will block* the heads.

### ☀ Tip
If you do block the heads, tell the skipper. It's not the end of the world, but it's quite embarrassing and not a very nice job to clear it. If it's your fault it is polite to volunteer to help.

# Electricity

## Electricity supply

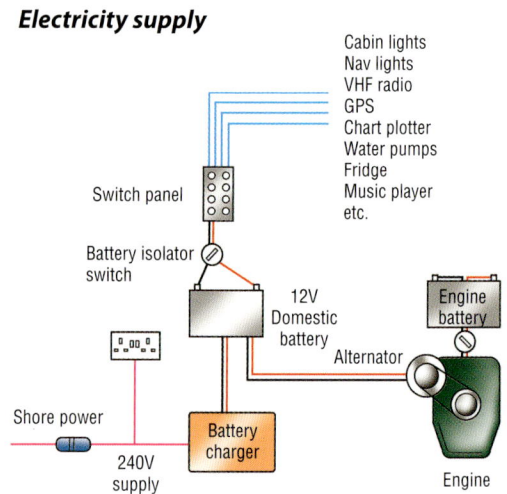

The electricity supply for a normal small to medium yacht is a couple of 12-volt batteries, similar to car batteries. The batteries are charged up by the **alternator** when the engine is running.

◆ The **engine battery**, for starting the engine, is normally kept separate so that you can start the engine if the other one is flat.

◆ The **domestic battery** is used for running the yacht's electric systems.

◆ Both batteries can be turned off with **isolator switches**.

Most yachts can plug into **shore power** when available, in marinas etc. This is a 240-volt supply, which runs:

◆ A battery charger on the yacht, to top up the batteries.

◆ Typically, a few normal domestic 13-amp sockets on the yacht.

◆ Anything else that needs 240 volts, eg TV or microwave.

There are other, less common arrangements. Some large yachts have **generators** to produce 240 volts on board, and some have **inverters** to run equipment such as televisions off the batteries.

### Using electricity

When *not* using shore power:

◆ Don't waste battery power. Turn lights off when not in use.
◆ Don't expect the 13-amp sockets to work (eg for chargers, hairdryers etc).
◆ Yachts with fridges tend not to run them all the time. Be aware of this, and don't leave them open.
◆ When running the engine, you can be more relaxed with battery-operated lights etc and can take the opportunity to run the fridge.

When using shore power these restrictions are unnecessary and the 13-amp sockets will work.

### Rubbish

Rubbish is collected in bags and stored so that it can be disposed of onshore: harbours and marinas have skips for rubbish, and some have recycling facilities.

◆ Pack the rubbish as tightly as possible (squash tins and cartons) so that it can be stored easily.
◆ Biodegradable material (leftover food) can be discarded at sea if well offshore, but this is not allowed in certain areas eg harbours.

# Sleeping

### Sleeping on board

Places to sleep are called **berths**. A narrow single berth is probably the most comfortable at sea, because you remain still when the boat heels over and moves around. Luxurious wide berths have greater appeal but work best when the yacht is tied up alongside.

Bring your own:

◆ Sleeping bag
◆ Pillow.

Keep your belongings stowed tidily. This is a good idea because:

◆ It allows you to find things.
◆ It prevents your stuff from getting wet.
◆ It means someone else can use the berth at sea.

All proper sea-going berths will have **lee cloths** – a sheet of strong material on the side of the berth that can be raised and tied to prevent you from falling out. It's important to use this even if the yacht is heeled over so as to roll you into the berth – the yacht may tack while you're asleep.

When on long passages, it is normal to sleep in off-watch periods during the day. For some of us, one of the most attractive things about sailing is that you can go to sleep during the day when others are on watch!

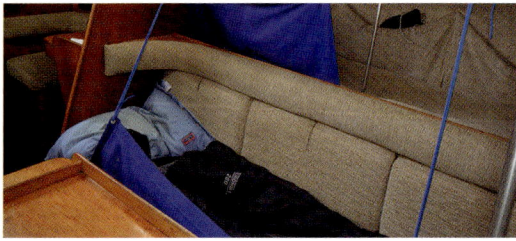

*All proper sea-going berths are equipped with lee cloths.*

### *Ropes and knots*

Sailing yachts use ropes for many purposes. You may find the profusion of ropes and lines confusing to begin with, but they make sense once you know what they are used for.

Crew need to know the names of some of the ropes and lines, so that you can understand what you are being asked to do. This section introduces the most important names – later sections on **Handling the Mainsail/ Headsail**, **Berthing** and **Mooring** explain more fully how they are used and what they do.

Crew also need to learn various rope handling skills. This section covers coiling, using a winch, securing a rope to a yacht's cleat, and seven knots, which are all you will need.

### Rope names

The ropes and lines are named according to *what they do*.

**Lines for controlling sails:**

| | |
|---|---|
| **Sheet** | Adjusts the angle of the sail by pulling on the sail's corner (clew), or on the boom in the case of the mainsail. The **mainsheet** controls the mainsail, the **jib sheets** control the jib, and so on. |
| **Halyard** | Hoists the sail up (and keeps it there). Halyards are also named after the sails they are used with: **main halyard**, **genoa halyard**, **spinnaker halyard** etc. |
| **Roller furling line** | Operates a roller furling system, to furl and unfurl the sail. Usually, on cruising yachts, this is the headsail. (Occasionally the mainsail also has a roller furling system, in the mast.) |
| **Topping lift** | Lifts the boom. It keeps the boom up when the mainsail isn't hoisted. |
| **Kicking strap** | Pulls the boom down, to adjust the shape of the mainsail. |
| **Outhaul** | This pulls the clew of the mainsail out along the boom, to adjust its shape. |
| **Reefing line** | There are generally two or three of these (**first reefing line**, **second reefing line** etc) and they are used to reef the mainsail (make it smaller), by pulling it down to the boom. |
| **Preventer** | This is attached to the boom when sailing downwind, to prevent the mainsail from gybing. |
| **Uphaul** | Holds the spinnaker pole up. |

**Downhaul** Holds the spinnaker pole down and forward.

**Guy** Pulls the spinnaker pole aft.

## Ropes for tying up the yacht:

**Warp** The name for any rope used to tie up a yacht.

**Bow line** A line attached to the bows, to hold the bows in.

**Stern line** A line attached to the stern, to hold the stern in.

**Bow spring** A line attached to the bows, or to a centre cleat, running to a shore cleat further aft. It prevents the yacht from moving forward.

**Stern spring** A line attached to the stern, or to a centre cleat, running to a shore cleat further forward. It prevents the yacht from moving aft.

**Shore line** When rafting on another yacht, shore lines are used to hold the bows and stern directly to the shore – bypassing the inner vessels.

**Breast line** A line from the centre of the yacht to hold it onto the pontoon/wall/neighbouring vessel (often a temporary arrangement for arriving or leaving).

**Mooring line** The line attaching the yacht to a mooring.

## Other ropes and lines:

**Painter** Line attached to the bows of a small boat eg a dinghy.

**Sail tie** Short piece of line used to tie sails in a bundle, etc.

# Coiling a rope

### *Coiling a rope*

Ropes need to be coiled neatly so that they can be stowed away, and undone again later, without getting muddled.

This illustration shows a rope being coiled. You hold the coils in one hand, and make the coils with the other. As each coil is formed, you give the rope a twist with your fingers so that the new coil hangs neatly, lying parallel to the others.

At the end the whole coil needs to be tied up so that it doesn't come undone. There are various methods for this (skippers will tell you their own preference). Below is a good secure method that will stay tied when the coiled rope is stored in a locker with other lines.

1. Wrap round the coil

2. Pass a loop through the coil

3. Push the loop back over the coil

4. And pull down, snug and secure

This figure shows a method that is more suitable for ropes that will be hung on a hook.

1. Wrap round the coil

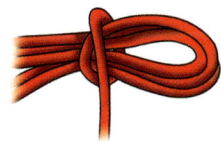

2. Pass a loop through the coil

3. Pass the end through the loop

4. Pull tight and hang up the coil

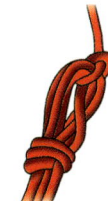

Here is a quick method that is commonly used to tidy up the long end of a sailing line. It can be undone quickly.

1. Coil the line

2. Pick up one loop and wrap it around the coil

3. Pull the wrap tight

4. And pass the loop through the coil.
   Hang it up

### The winch

Winches are used to pull ropes. They are a very useful way of putting a lot of tension on lines attached to sails that (sometimes) need to be very tight, like sheets or halyards.

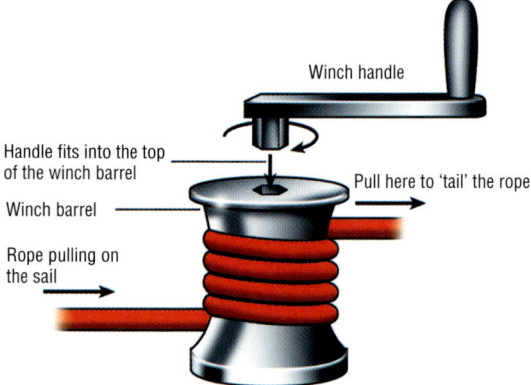

Winch handle

Handle fits into the top of the winch barrel

Pull here to 'tail' the rope

Winch barrel

Rope pulling on the sail

The key to a winch is the friction between the rope and the barrel, which allows the winch to grip the rope. This is why you wrap the rope round the barrel several times.

The barrel of the winch only turns one way – clockwise. You wind the rope round the winch clockwise. The more rope turns there are on the winch, the more tension you can put on the rope. Start at the bottom, and make sure the turns don't overlap each other.

> ✴ **Tip**
> If you have difficulty remembering which way to wrap the rope, simply give the winch a twist before you put the rope on. Wind the rope round in the same direction as the winch turns.

Once the turns are on, pull in any slack and then, ideally, one person keeps the tension on the loose end of the rope (this is called **tailing** the rope) while another person puts the **winch handle** in and winds it.

✳ **Tip**
Position yourself over the winch as you wind. This makes turning the handle easier.

There is often more than one gear on a large winch. If you wind the handle clockwise, the winch barrel generally turns at the same speed as the handle. Then, if you wind it anticlockwise the barrel goes slower, so you can pull the rope in with greater force.

When you have finished winching, the tension still needs to be kept on the end of the rope; otherwise the turns will slip. Keep the tension on with your hand, take a turn round a cleat and make it fast (see page 26).

✳ **Tip**
When the rope turns on the winch overlap each other, it is called a **riding turn**. If you get a riding turn, stop winching, take the turns off and sort it out immediately. If you carry on winching, it will get completely jammed.

# The winch

### Self-tailing winches

Some winches have a **self-tailer** attached. This grips the loose end of the rope and makes it easier to operate the winch on your own, without somebody tailing the line. The self-tailer keeps the tension on the rope when you have stopped winching.

> ✳ **Tip**
> For safety, you can put an extra loose turn round the winch when you've stopped so the rope doesn't get knocked out of the self-tailer by accident.

### Extra turns

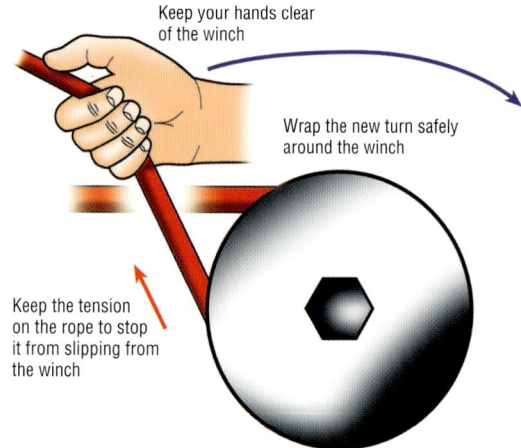

Keep your hands clear of the winch

Wrap the new turn safely around the winch

Keep the tension on the rope to stop it from slipping from the winch

Sometimes you start winching with, say, three turns on and then you realise you need another turn to get more tension. See above for the safe way of putting an extra turn on when the rope is under tension.

**NO!**

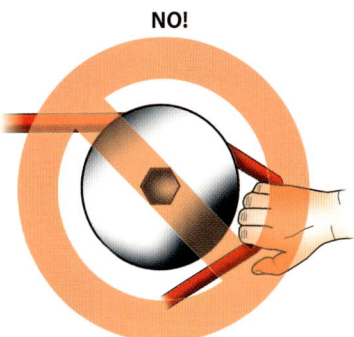

*Never* get your fingers between the rope and the winch barrel – if the rope slips on the winch, your fingers would be painfully trapped.

## Easing the line

Press your hand flat onto the turns so that the rope still grips onto the winch barrel. Hold the tail of the rope loosely and ease the turns round the barrel.

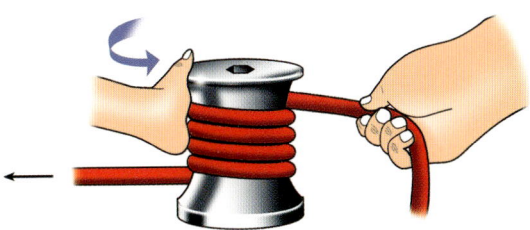

This shows how you **ease** a line, i.e. let just a little rope out to reduce the tension – eg when adjusting a sheet. Press the flat of you hand on the turns and ease them slowly back round the winch (while watching for the effect on the sail shape). For safety, keep your controlling hand well away from where the line feeds onto the winch.

# Cleats

### *Cleating off a rope*

Cleats are used on boats and on pontoons to hold ropes tightly. The simplest and quickest way of making a rope fast on a cleat is:

◆ One turn completely round the cleat.
◆ One 'figure-of-eight' on the cleat.
◆ A final complete turn round the cleat and pull tight (so that the last turn wedges itself under the earlier turns).

1. One full turn round the cleat

2. 'Figure of eight' turn

3. Another full turn around

4. And pull tight

The only time you may need more than this is if you have a small rope on a large cleat. In that case, double up: use two complete turns and then two figure-of-eights.

Although it's true that the more turns you have the more secure it is, the above method is adequate, and is quick to do and – just as importantly – undo. And you will probably have room to make another rope off on the same cleat if you need to.

### Locking turns

If you are leaving a yacht secured for an extended time, put an extra turn of the warp on the cleat for added security – and you can also finish off

with a **locking turn**. This is more secure: if the rope slips slightly, the locking turn tightens up.

---

**✳ Tip**

Most skippers dislike locking turns on lines that control the sails because:

◆ They are unnecessary.
◆ These working lines usually need to be undone quickly and easily, and a locking turn can go very tight.

---

*Crew are winching and tailing.*

# Knots

Out of the many hundreds of knots and hitches available, the following are all you really need on a sailing boat.

## *Figure-of-eight*

1. Twist the rope to form a loop

2. Pass the end over, then up through the loop

3. 'Figure of eight' pulled tight

◆ A simple stopper knot that can be used on the end of lines so that they can't slip back through jammers or turning blocks.

In particular, the headsail sheet generally has this knot tied at its end. This knot doesn't pull too tight, and is easy to undo.

> ✳ **Tip**
> It is said that there have probably been more lives lost as a result of using a reef knot (see opposite) as a bend (i.e. to tie two ropes together) than from the failure of any other half dozen knots combined. You have been warned!

### *Reef knot (square knot)*

1. Start off like tying
   your shoelaces

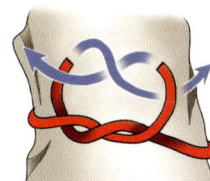

2. Pull tight, then tie the
   ends again

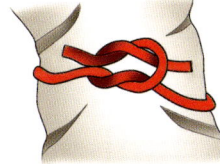

3. Reef knot pulled tight

◆ Most common use: to tie up a bundle of sail.

This knot is only secure when it lies against something. It is a good knot to use for this, because you can easily tie something up reasonably tightly.

*Never* use a reef knot as a *bend* – i.e. to tie two ropes together. It is very insecure, particularly if the ropes are different sizes.

# Knots

## *Clove hitch*

1. Pass the end over the rail, then back under to one side of the line

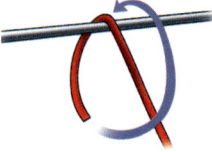

2. Then over again on the other side of the line

3. And back through the loop you made

4. Clove hitch pulled tight

◆ Clove hitch: useful for attaching fenders to a guardrail.

The clove hitch is quick to tie and easy to adjust, eg to get the fenders to the right height. It is also reasonably secure. You can add a half hitch when the fenders have been checked and adjusted before leaving them.

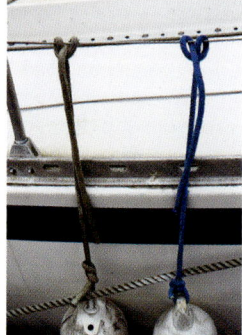

## Rolling hitch

1. Pass the end over the rail, then back under to one side of the line

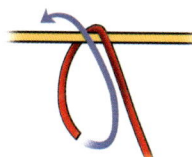

2. Then over again on the same side of the line

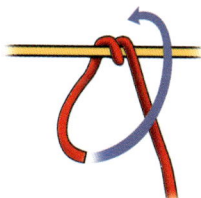

3. Then over again on the other side of the line, and back through the loop you made

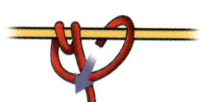

4. Rolling hitch pulled tight

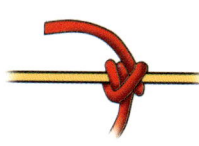

◆ Rolling hitch: used for gripping another line.

The rolling hitch grips when it is pulled *along* the line it is tied to. It is very effective for taking the tension off another line, for example if you need some slack in order to free a riding turn on a winch. Or it can be used when you want to attach a warp to the anchor chain, to transfer the load to the warp (which can reduce the noise from the chain).

# Knots

### *Round turn and two half hitches*

1. Round turn

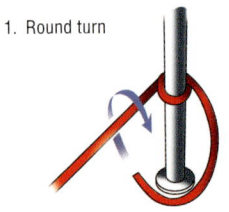

2. First half hitch

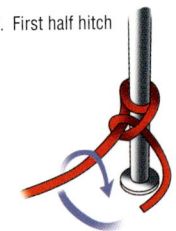

3. Second half hitch

4. Pull tight

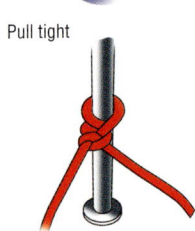

◆ Used for tying a warp or dinghy painter to a cleat, pole or ring ashore. (The round turn can pass through the middle of the cleat – this is more secure and takes up less room on the cleat.)

Though marginally less secure than a bowline (see page 34) this knot has the advantage that it can be tied and untied when the warp is under tension. Once you take a turn round the object in question, it makes it easier to hold the load on the warp – and then it's very quick to finish off with two half hitches.

## ✳ Tip

If you want to learn knots (the bowline in particular), don't just do them when you go sailing. Keep a length of rope at home and *practise* – you can do it while watching TV.

## *Sheet bend, single and double*

1. Form a loop in the larger line. Pass the smaller line through the loop

2. Take the small line to one side and under the big loop

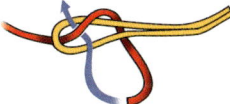

3. Then back across the top of the loop going under itself

4. Single sheet bend

5. Turn it into a double sheet bend by going round the big loop again

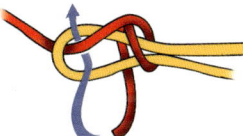

6. And under itself again

7. Double sheet bend pulled tight

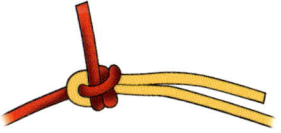

◆ A secure knot to tie two ropes together.

It is useful when, for example, you want to make a longer warp to use as a shore line. It even works if the two ropes are of different sizes: form the initial loop using the thicker rope.

The double sheet bend is a bit more secure than the single one.

### *Bowline*

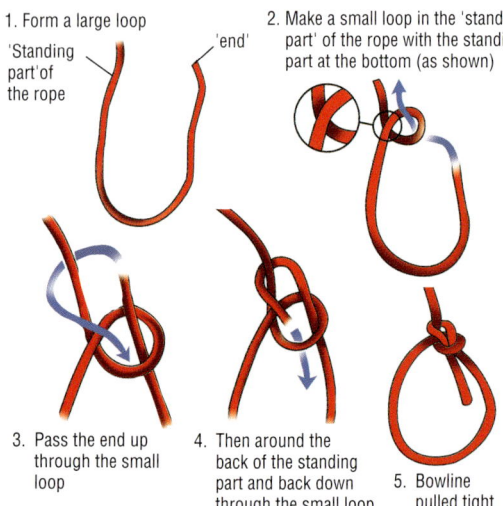

1. Form a large loop

'Standing part' of the rope

'end'

2. Make a small loop in the 'standing part' of the rope with the standing part at the bottom (as shown)

3. Pass the end up through the small loop

4. Then around the back of the standing part and back down through the small loop

5. Bowline pulled tight

◆ Used to tie a loop.

The bowline can be a bit of a challenge for beginners to tie, but it is simple enough when learned. It is a very secure loop for a number of uses on a yacht, eg attaching sheets to the headsail, securing a warp to a large bollard. For security, leave a reasonably long tail.

A tight bowline can be undone by pushing the top loop away from the main loop as shown below.

1. Tight bowline – top view

2. View from the side. Bend the standing part back, and push the top of the knot over, as shown

3. It is now easy to loosen the knot

Yachts rely on their engines to manoeuvre up to their berths, and at sea when there is no wind. The engine also drives an alternator to charge the batteries. Yacht engines are usually diesel.

## The engine control

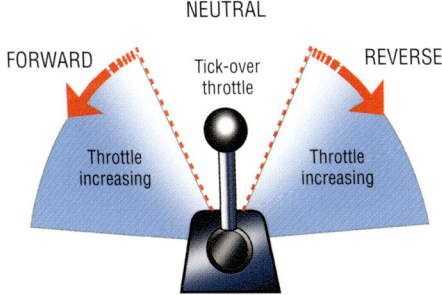

Engine controls vary and the skipper will explain how the yacht's particular control works. The diagram shows a typical design.

◆ Upright position: drive is in neutral and the engine speed is at tick-over.
◆ Push the lever forward: the propeller is engaged in forward. Move it further forward and the engine speed increases.
◆ Pull the lever back: the propeller is engaged in reverse. Move it further back for increased engine speed.
◆ Sometimes you need a bit of throttle in neutral, i.e. without engaging the propeller. This is usually done by operating a button, then pushing the lever forward.

# The engine

### *Starting the engine*

Getting ready:

◆ The skipper does routine engine checks, generally once a day before starting.

◆ Turn on the **engine battery** at the **isolator switch**.

◆ If the engine has a pull lever for stopping, make sure it is pushed in.

◆ If the fuel is routinely turned off, turn it on.

◆ Make sure the seacock for the seawater cooling supply is open.

Then:

◆ On the engine control, disengage the gears and set to about half throttle.

◆ Turn on the electric key switch, and operate the **pre-heat** (generally for about 15 seconds).

◆ Operate the starter switch until the engine starts.

◆ Check that water is coming out of the exhaust. If it is not (the exhaust will sound dry and 'trumpety') stop the engine at once and tell the skipper.

*The photo shows a typical engine control.*

To warm up the engine, run in neutral with a bit of throttle.

> ✳ **Tip**
> If the engine fails to start, do not keep operating the starter motor – this will only run the battery down. Stop, and tell the skipper.

> ✳ **Tip**
> When moving into gear, do the first bit *positively* – you will feel and hear a sort of 'thump' when the gear engages, initially with slow engine speed. After that, *gradually* move the lever further for increased throttle and speed.
>
> Don't go quickly from forward to reverse and vice versa. Make a positive move to neutral, and then another positive move into the other gear.

### Stopping the engine

◆ Put the engine control to neutral.
◆ If the engine is equipped with a **stop button**, or **lever**, operate this to stop the engine.
◆ Turn off the key (with some engines, this will stop the engine).
◆ Turn off the battery isolator switch (this prevents the battery from being discharged).
◆ When sailing, it may be necessary to put the engine control into reverse so that the propeller doesn't spin with the motion through the water.

### Steering under engine

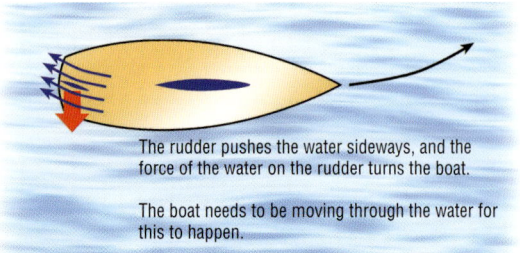

The rudder pushes the water sideways, and the force of the water on the rudder turns the boat.

The boat needs to be moving through the water for this to happen.

A yacht is steered by a **rudder**. Depending on the type of yacht, the rudder is controlled either by a **wheel** or by a **tiller**. In either case, the steering device is called the **helm** and steering is known as **helming**.

The yacht needs to be moving through the water in order to steer. If it is stationary in the water the helm will have no effect (apart from prop wash off the rudder – see page 43).

### Going forwards

Once the yacht is moving forward through the water, it can be turned with the rudder.

◆ With a wheel, turn clockwise – top to the right – to steer to starboard, i.e. just like a car.

◆ With a tiller, push the tiller to port to turn the yacht to starboard.

◆ If you keep the rudder in its central position, the yacht will go in a straight line.

If you are moving quickly through the water, you won't need much helm to turn the yacht. When moving slowly you will need more helm and the yacht will turn more slowly.

Using a lot of helm slows the yacht down.

**YACHT UNDER MOTOR**

*The helmsman is steering with a wheel.*

### Steering in a straight line

Pick a point on the horizon and keep the bows lined up against that point. Watch the bows carefully, and try to find the position of the wheel or tiller that keeps the bows still against the horizon. Make small corrections to stop the movement to port or starboard.

Ideally, you should be able to steer in a straight line with *very little movement* of the helm.

If you are steering a compass course, don't try to steer purely by the compass. First get onto the correct course, then *look up* to see which way the bows are pointing and find a point to steer towards. From time to time look down at the compass again to see if you need to adjust the course.

**✳ Tip**

If you make too much helm movement, you will start 'oversteering' – steering too far one way and then too far the other to correct it, so that the yacht follows an S-shaped course. Look back at the wake to see if it's straight.

## Steering under engine

### *Steering astern*

There are two important differences when steering **astern** (moving backwards through the water).

◆ The helm works the other way round. So to turn the bows to starboard:
  ○ Turn the wheel anticlockwise, or top to the left.
  ○ Pull the tiller to starboard.

◆ The force of the water on the rudder will try to push the wheel or tiller to its limit. Grip the helm tightly to prevent this.

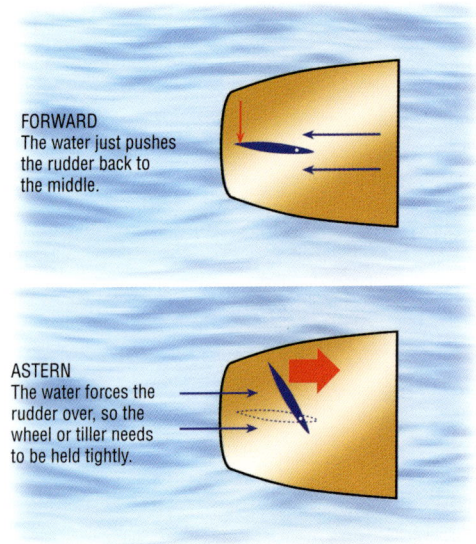

FORWARD
The water just pushes the rudder back to the middle.

ASTERN
The water forces the rudder over, so the wheel or tiller needs to be held tightly.

If possible, go slowly. The force on the helm will be less and the manoeuvre more controlled if you go slowly through the water. Put the gear into neutral if the yacht is picking up too much speed.

## ✳ Tip

When steering astern, it is less confusing if you turn round and face the stern, with the tiller or wheel in front of you (with a wheel, stand on the 'wrong' side of the binnacle, or to the side of it, facing aft).

◆ With a wheel, you then steer in the direction you want to go, like driving a car (but grip the wheel tightly).
◆ When using a tiller, simply point the tiller in the direction you want to go.

Remember, it is the yacht's *movement through the water* that determines how you should steer, not whether you are in forward or reverse gear. If you are moving astern and you then put the engine into forward, you will still be *moving astern through the water* for a few seconds, while the yacht slows down. So keep steering astern (or keep the helm central) until the yacht starts moving forward.

*Steering astern: the helmsman is pointing the tiller in the required direction.*

# Manoeuvring

### *Prop walk*

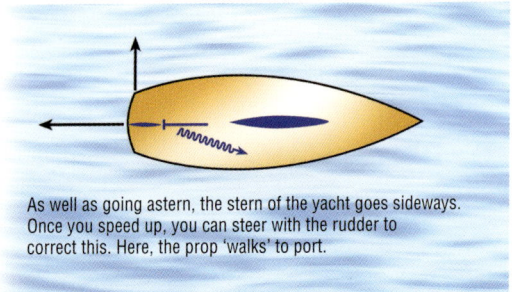

As well as going astern, the stern of the yacht goes sideways. Once you speed up, you can steer with the rudder to correct this. Here, the prop 'walks' to port.

When you start to reverse a yacht, the stern will tend to go sideways a bit: it will 'walk' to port or starboard. Different yachts go different ways, but an individual yacht will always 'walk' in the same direction.

The skipper should be able to tell you which way the stern will 'walk', or you can see for yourself once you start reversing. When the yacht speeds up a bit, you can steer to correct the 'walk'.

*The yacht is motoring through a marina.*

### *Prop wash off the rudder*

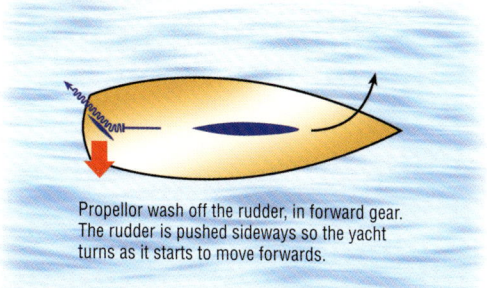

Propellor wash off the rudder, in forward gear.
The rudder is pushed sideways so the yacht
turns as it starts to move forwards.

Most yachts have their propellers just in front of the rudder, so you can turn the yacht a bit when it is stationary in the water:

◆ Put the helm hard over.
◆ Give a strong *forward* burst with the throttle.

You will be able to feel the force of the propeller wash on the rudder, and this force will turn the yacht. This can be useful in tight spaces.

✷ **Tip**

A yacht can be turned almost in its own length by using a combination of prop walk and prop wash off the rudder.

◆ Turn the yacht the way that will be assisted by the prop walk (i.e. clockwise in the above diagram, where the walk is to port).
◆ Keep the rudder hard over.
◆ Use short bursts of throttle forward and astern.

Ask your skipper to demonstrate this.

## Sail trim

### *How sails work*

The flow of air over correctly positioned sails produces 'lift' like an aerofoil. This provides the sailing yacht's propulsion. If the sails are pulled (sheeted) too far in, the air cannot flow over the outside of the sail. Similarly, if the sails are eased too much they will just flap, flag-like, in the wind.

**View of the sail from the top**

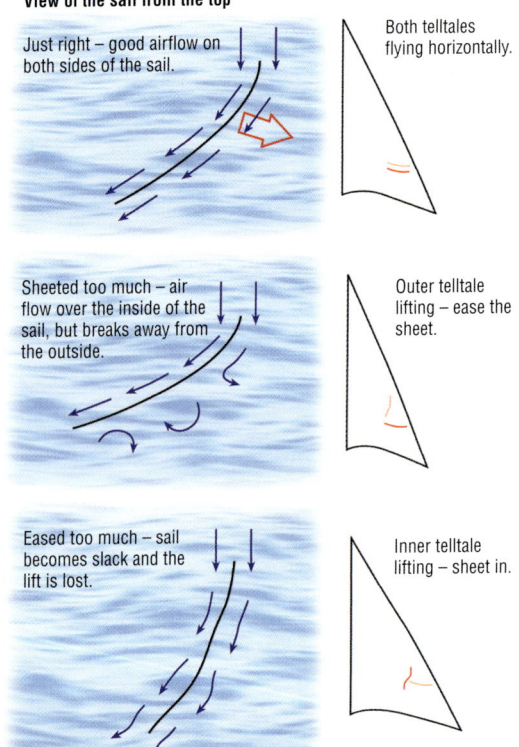

Just right – good airflow on both sides of the sail.

Both telltales flying horizontally.

Sheeted too much – air flow over the inside of the sail, but breaks away from the outside.

Outer telltale lifting – ease the sheet.

Eased too much – sail becomes slack and the lift is lost.

Inner telltale lifting – sheet in.

### Trimming the sails

When you are sailing, you adjust the sails according to where the wind is coming from. This is known as **trimming** the sails.

A headsail (jib or genoa) often has **telltales** (little strips of material stuck to the sail), which help you to see the air flow over the sail. On a correctly adjusted sail, the telltails on both sides of the sail fly horizontal, parallel to the flow of wind. If it's not correctly adjusted, the telltales flap around and go up vertically.

◆ If the telltale on the *outside* of the sail is lifting, ease the sheet (*central figure*).
◆ If the telltale on the *inside* is lifting, sheet in (*bottom figure*).

With the mainsail, look at the area near the luff. When correctly adjusted, this should look slack (lifting slightly) which indicates that it is pointing straight into the wind. Telltales attached to the leech should be flying horizontally out from the sail.

◆ If the sail looks tight right up to the mast, ease the sheet.
◆ If the sail is flapping, sheet in.

> ✳ **Tip**
> As well a adjusting the sheets, the shape of the headsail and mainsail can be trimmed to suit the conditions, by changing the position of the sheet car and mainsail sheet traveller, and by adjusting the outhaul, halyard and kicking strap tension. These can have a significant effect on the yacht's speed. It's interesting to try these adjustments (with the skipper's advice), to see what results they have.

## Points of sail

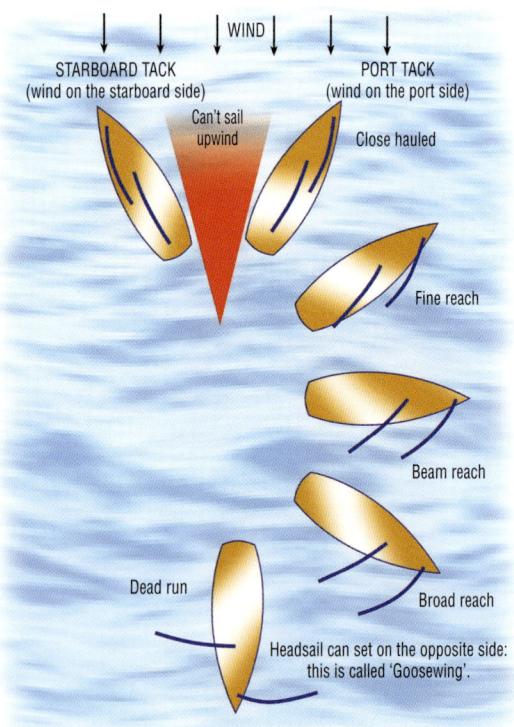

WIND

STARBOARD TACK
(wind on the starboard side)

PORT TACK
(wind on the port side)

Can't sail upwind

Close hauled

Fine reach

Beam reach

Dead run

Broad reach

Headsail can set on the opposite side:
this is called 'Goosewing'.

Sailors have expressions to describe where the wind is coming from, relative to the yacht: for example, from the port or starboard side of the yacht, from near the bow, or from behind.

These different wind directions are known as **points of sail**. The above diagram shows the commonly used points of sail.

### Coming up to wind

When the yacht alters course towards the direction of the wind, the sails have to be sheeted in.

Headsail:

◆ Uncleat the end of the sheet, and keep some tension on it (i.e. tail it).

◆ With a self-tailing winch, keep the sheet in the self-tailer.

◆ Put in the winch handle and turn it.

Mainsail:

◆ Pull (or winch) the mainsheet in.

This process is known as **hardening up**.

> ☀ **Tip**
> Watch both sails for the correct adjustment as you are trimming them. For really efficient sailing, you should make these trimming adjustments *while the yacht is changing course.* The idea is to keep the sails correctly trimmed while the yacht is turning.

### Bearing away

When the yacht alters course away from the wind, the sheets on all sails have to be eased.

Headsail:

◆ Uncleat the end of the sheet, or remove it from the self-tailer, and hold it to keep the tension on it.

◆ Place the other hand flat against the turns on the winch.

◆ Ease the sheet gradually round the winch, while watching the shape of the sail.

Mainsail:

◆ Release the mainsheet from its jammer.

◆ Gradually ease the sheet until the luff just lifts.

This process is known as **freeing off**.

### *Tacking*

This is when a yacht turns its bows through the wind, so that the wind comes onto the opposite side of the boat.

Generally, the yacht will be on a close reach or close-hauled before a tack, with the sails sheeted in. During the tack both sails need to move across, and after it the wind will be on the opposite side of the sails.

◆ Mainsail: the boom swings across and no action is required by the crew. It may need to be trimmed after the tack, when the yacht is on its new course.
◆ Headsail: the crew need to take action to:
  ❍ release the sheet which was holding the sail in position before the tack,
  ❍ allow (or assist) the sail to move round the mast, and
  ❍ sheet it in on the opposite side.

There are two sheets attached to a headsail, and when sailing one of them is **working** and the other is known

*The crew work together to tack the yacht.*

as the **lazy** sheet. During a tack, the working sheet is released and becomes the lazy sheet and the lazy sheet is winched in to become the working sheet.

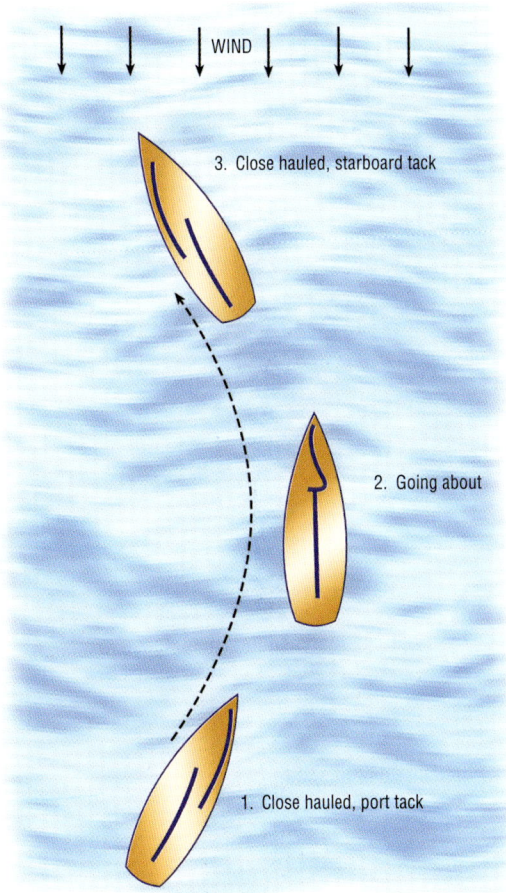

WIND

3. Close hauled, starboard tack

2. Going about

1. Close hauled, port tack

# Tacking

## CREW ACTIONS FOR TACKING

With a big crew, you will be given a specific job, eg on the port or starboard headsail sheet, the mainsheet, or the helm. The skipper will tell the crew what each person is supposed to do.

◆ Helm calls 'Ready about!'
◆ Lazy sheet: take two turns round the winch, pull in the slack and call 'Ready!'
◆ Working sheet: release from cleat or self-tailer, holding it under tension, call 'Ready!'
◆ Helm turns the yacht through the wind and calls, 'Lee-oh!'; then settles the yacht on the new course.
◆ Working sheet/new lazy sheet: unwind from the winch and let it run. Make sure it stays free to run (watch out for kinks going into the turning block).
◆ Lazy sheet/new working sheet: pull in by hand until the sail is round the mast, then when you start putting tension on the sail get another turn on the winch. Put the winch handle in, and one crew tails while the other turns the winch handle (or put the sheet in the self-tailer).
◆ Keep winching the sail in until it is trimmed.
◆ Mainsail: trim as necessary. If the mainsheet block needs to be moved up or down the track, this can be done before or during the tack.
◆ With a large genoa, it may help if crew on the foredeck assist the sail round the mast and 'skirt' it over the guardrail.

### Gybing

This is when the yacht turns so that the stern goes through the wind – the wind is coming from behind the yacht. As with tacking, the wind will come onto the opposite side of the boat, and both sails will switch sides.

Generally, before and after the gybe, the yacht will be on a broad reach or dead run – with both mainsail and headsail eased right out.

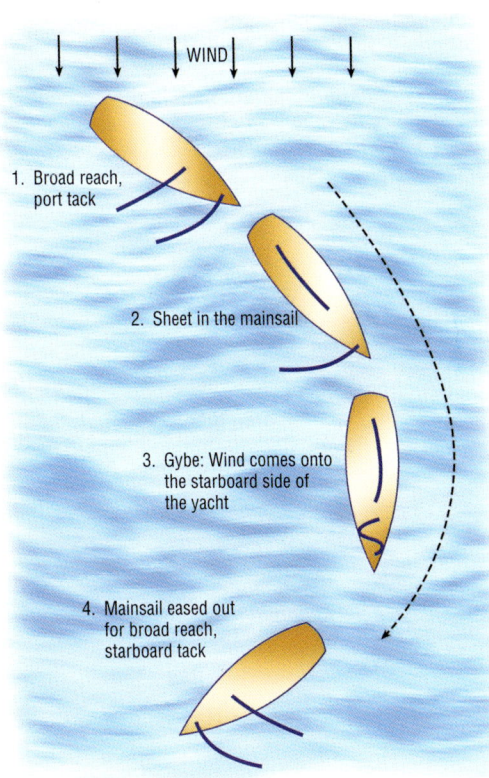

WIND

1. Broad reach, port tack

2. Sheet in the mainsail

3. Gybe: Wind comes onto the starboard side of the yacht

4. Mainsail eased out for broad reach, starboard tack

# Gybing

◆ Mainsail: before the gybe begins, the mainsail needs to be sheeted in hard, so that the sail and boom are secured tightly to the centre of the yacht. Once the turn is completed, and the wind is on the opposite side of the sail, it is eased right out.

◆ Headsail: as the stern of the yacht turns through the wind, the sail will move across – it is controlled into its new position by easing one sheet and taking up on the other. The lazy sheet becomes the working sheet and vice versa.

*It is absolutely essential to sheet the mainsail right in to the centre of the yacht and secure it before the gybe.*

*If this is not done, the boom will crash from one side to the other, with the full force of the wind on the mainsail. This can cause serious damage to the yacht, and injury to the crew.*

*For this reason, gybing is a more dangerous manoeuvre than tacking.*

## CREW ACTIONS FOR A CONTROLLED GYBE

The skipper will give you a specific job to do, eg on the port or starboard headsail sheet, the mainsheet or the helm, and will tell you what you are supposed to do.

◆ Helm: calls 'Ready to gybe!'
◆ Mainsheet: pull it in quickly, right to the centre of the yacht and secure it in the jammer. When it's tightly secured, call 'Ready!'
◆ Headsail: one crew controls each sheet. To get ready, take the working sheet off the cleat or self-tailer, and take up any slack on the lazy sheet. Hold each sheet with two turns round the winch.
◆ Helm: turns so that the stern goes through the wind. When the wind comes onto the opposite side of the mainsail *and not before*, call 'Gybe-oh!' Take care to keep the yacht turning (i.e. don't gybe back again) and settle onto the new course.
◆ Mainsheet: ease it all the way out.
◆ Headsail: control the clew with the two sheets until the sail stays on the 'new' side of the yacht – then release the (now) lazy sheet (allow it to run freely) and trim the sail with the new working sheet.

Everyone should keep well out of the way of the *boom* (heads down!) and the *mainsheet* during the gybe, in case wind catches the mainsail before it is fully sheeted in.

## Steering under sail

### *Steering under sail*

The helm of a yacht under sail is an integral part of the balance of forces of wind and water that propel the yacht. The wheel or tiller will have an entirely different feel to it than when motoring.

Generally speaking, a light force will need to be applied through the helm to keep the yacht sailing on course. This is called **weather helm**.

Weather helm requires you to hold the yacht *away from the wind*. If you let go of the helm, the yacht will round up into the wind (or **luff up**) – and stop, with the sails flapping.

◆ On a starboard tack (wind from the starboard side) you will need to apply the light force on the wheel or tiller to 'turn to port' in order to keep the yacht going straight.
◆ On a port tack, the helm will need to be held to starboard.

> ✳ **Tip**
> With a tiller, sit on the weather side of the cockpit (the 'high' side when the yacht is heeled over) and keep the tiller pulled towards you.

The force required on the helm is not constant. Weather helm increases in gusts and reduces in calms, waves push the yacht to one side or the other, and you need to compensate for these things when they happen, to keep the yacht on course.

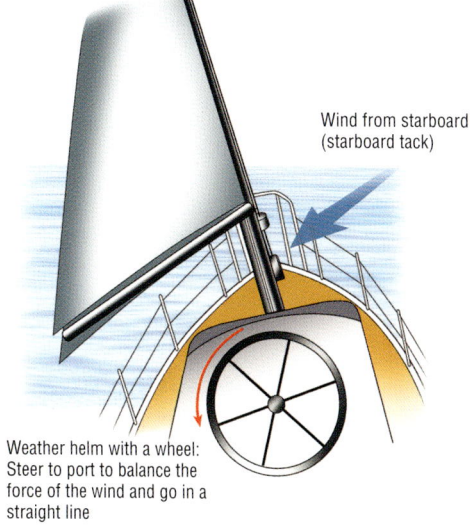

Wind from starboard
(starboard tack)

Weather helm with a wheel:
Steer to port to balance the
force of the wind and go in a
straight line

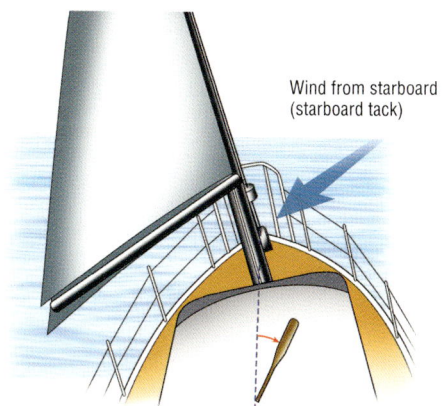

Wind from starboard
(starboard tack)

Weather helm with a tiller: Pull the tiller towards the wind to
balance the force of the wind and go in a straight line

# Steering under sail

## *Compass course or close-hauled?*

When steering a yacht at sea, there are two possible situations:

◆ The wind direction is such that you can sail straight towards your destination. So the navigator works out the course, and the helmsman steers that course by the compass.

◆ Alternatively, your destination is upwind so you cannot sail directly towards it. In that case the helmsman steers as close to the wind as the yacht will sail. He then tells the navigator the best heading the yacht is able to make, and at some stage you will need to tack. This is known as **beating** to windward.

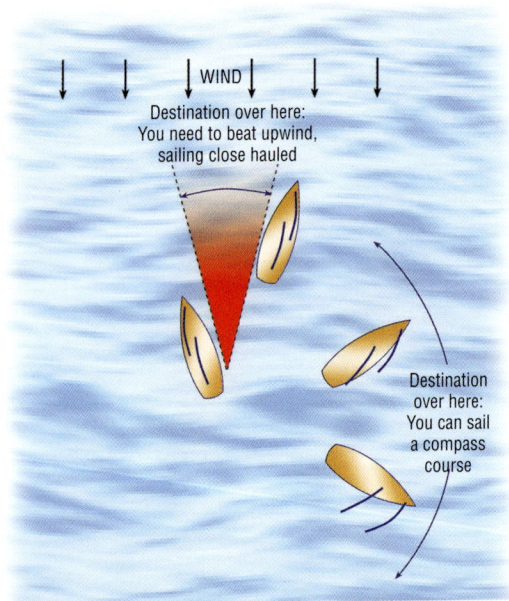

WIND

Destination over here:
You need to beat upwind,
sailing close hauled

Destination
over here:
You can sail
a compass
course

### How to steer a compass course

◆ Balance the weather helm so that the yacht sails in a straight line.

◆ Then give more port or starboard helm to get onto the correct course – as indicated by the steering compass.

◆ Once you're on the correct course, pick a spot on the horizon or a cloud in the sky, and keep the bows or forestay lined up with that.

◆ Make small helm adjustments if the bows move away from the mark, and find the helm position that keeps the bows steady.

◆ Trim the sails for this course.

◆ From time to time glance back at the compass to make sure you are on the right course.

◆ Keep an eye on the sail trim. If the wind changes direction, the crew will need to adjust the sails. The yacht stays on the same compass course, and the sails are kept in the optimum position for the wind direction.

> ✳ **Tip**
>
> To get onto the desired compass course, it is best to have a rough idea of the direction it corresponds to, eg so that you could point to it. Steer to that initially, then correct your course with the accurate numbers on the compass.
>
> For example, if you are told to steer 229°, that's roughly south-west, so you know it's 'over there'. Steer that way initially, and then correct it. Too many people bury their heads in the compass, and then steer the wrong way by misinterpreting the numbers. The delay of the compass swing doesn't help either.

### *How to steer close-hauled*

This time you are steering by the wind and sails, not by the compass.

◆ Steer as close to the wind as you can, with the sails fully sheeted in.

◆ If there is a wind indicator, you will find that a particular angle to the wind – usually about 40° – will give the best speed close-hauled. Note this, and use the wind indicator to help steer the yacht at the best angle.

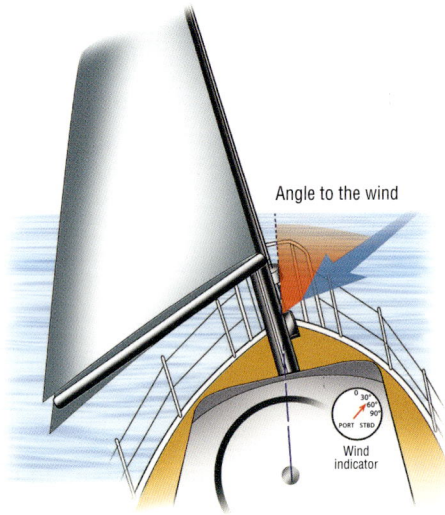

Angle to the wind

Wind indicator

---

**✳ Tip**

In light conditions you generally need to ease the sheets and outhaul, and may not be able to sail quite so close to the wind.

◆ The 'proof of the pudding' is speed through the water – keep an eye on the speed indicator, and see what makes the speed pick up or drop off.

◆ Go too close to the wind and the speed will drop off rapidly. Too far off the wind and you aren't sailing in the best direction. If the sails start flapping, you are too close to the wind, so steer away quickly before the yacht loses speed.

Try to make only small helm corrections, particularly in light conditions. Large movements of the rudder will slow the yacht down.

Once you are steady on the best course, you can tell the navigator what compass course you can achieve. This may change with time.

---

**✳ Tip**

Helming close-hauled requires concentration, and you can use several techniques to help you:

◆ You can steer by the telltails on the headsail, keeping both the outer and inner one flying horizontal.

◆ Keep an eye on the bows and a point on the horizon, to make sure the yacht keeps going straight.

---

**✳ Tip**

If you need to steer past something in the water, it is normally best to go downwind of it and clear it rather than 'pinch' and try to get past on the upwind side. If you pinch, the yacht will loose speed and leeway will increase – making it harder to get past the object. You may also need to consider which direction the tide is running: if in doubt, ask the skipper.

### Sailing downwind

You need to take particular care when sailing downwind, because it is easy (and dangerous) to gybe inadvertently.

◆ If you are helming on a broad reach, take particular care not to allow the yacht to swing further downwind, especially if there is a following sea (which may occasionally push the yacht off course).

◆ Always fix in your mind which way to steer to 'avoid the gybe'. This is also the way to steer to come up to the wind and do a crash stop, eg for Man Overboard. It is, in fact, the *safe way* to steer in any eventuality (eg if you have to alter course to avoid something).

Broad reach, port tack: Steer this way to avoid gybe

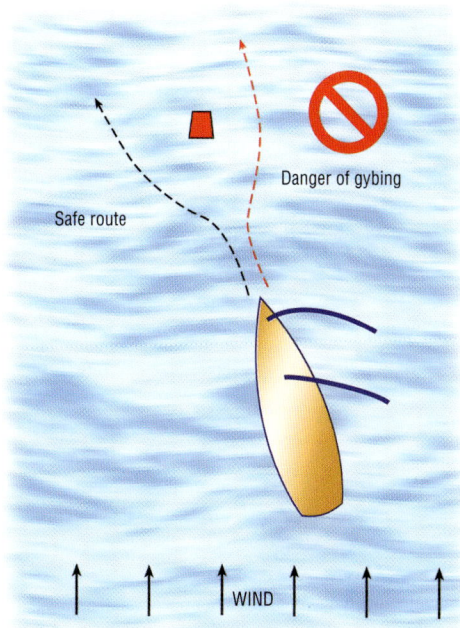

◆ If there is any danger of an inadvertent gybe – when on a broad reach or dead run for any length of time – a **preventer** should be fitted. Don't be afraid to suggest this if you are helming – it will make your job a lot more relaxed.

# Sailing downwind

### *The preventer*

A preventer is a strong line that is attached to the boom, and rigged so that it prevents the boom from moving if the yacht gybes accidentally. If the wind comes onto the back of the mainsail, the preventer will stop it from gybing. The yacht can then be steered back on course.

There are many ways to fit a preventer, and different yachts/skippers may have special tackle set up to make it easier to fit and remove.

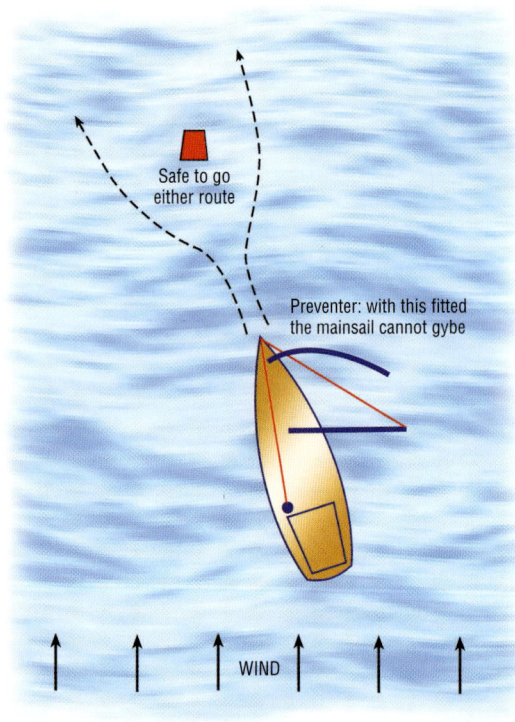

Safe to go either route

Preventer: with this fitted the mainsail cannot gybe

WIND

In its simplest version the preventer is attached to the end of the boom, run to a point well forward on the yacht (eg through a bow fairlead) and back to a winch or cleat where it can be tensioned and secured. It is best for the preventer to be secured at the cockpit, so that it can be released quickly if needed. The following instructions apply to this simple version.

> ✷ **Tip**
> If the mainsail tries to gybe, the force on the preventer will be considerable. Attaching to the end of the boom, and to a strong point as far forward as possible, gives the best arrangement for a safe, effective preventer.

### CREW ACTIONS TO FIT A PREVENTER
◆ With the boom sheeted in, tie the end of a long line (a warp is suitable) to a secure point at the end of the boom – use a long bowline loop so it can be reached and untied easily.
◆ Someone takes the other end forward, on the lee-side deck, passing the line outside everything eg shrouds and headsail sheet.

> ✷ **Tip**
> Rather than carry a coil of rope up the side deck unwinding it as you go, it is easier if the person going forward just holds the end of the line, and someone else pays it out from the cockpit.

◆ Bring the end of the line in through the fairlead at the lee bow, and then straight back to the cockpit.

## Sailing downwind

◆ Put the line on a winch. Ease the mainsheet and allow the boom to move out for the correct sail trim, taking up the slack on the preventer. When the boom is in position, secure the sheet, then tension the preventer with the winch. Secure the tail of the preventer on a cleat or self-tailer.

When it's correctly set up, the boom is held firmly in position with the preventer pulling it out and the sheet pulling it in.

If you need to come up to wind quickly (eg to change course or for a crash stop) just release the end of the preventer from the cleat and winch, and pull in the mainsheet.

A preventer rigged this way will need to be removed before a tack or gybe, and reset afterwards.

### CREW ACTIONS TO REMOVE THE PREVENTER
◆ Release the end of the preventer from the cleat/winch.
◆ Sheet in the mainsail until you can reach the boom.
◆ Untie the preventer bowline from the boom.
◆ Pull the other end to bring the line back into the cockpit, preferably without it going into the water.

#### ✳ Tip
If you are removing the preventer prior to gybing, make sure the mainsail is fully sheeted in first.

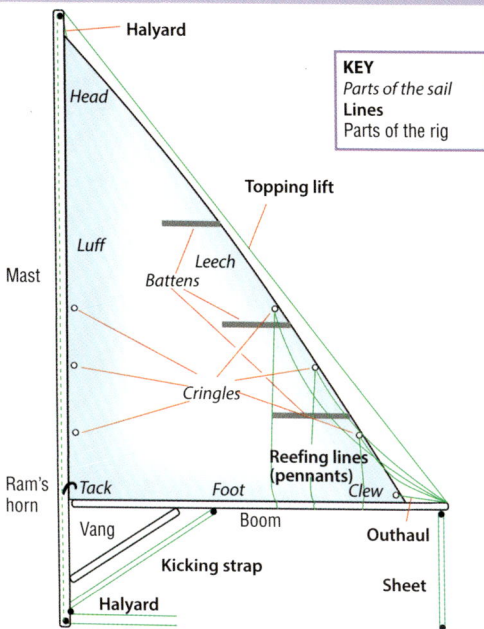

KEY
*Parts of the sail*
**Lines**
Parts of the rig

Halyard

Head

Topping lift

Luff

Leech

Battens

Mast

Cringles

Reefing lines
(pennants)

Ram's horn

Tack

Foot

Clew

Vang

Boom

Outhaul

Kicking strap

Sheet

Halyard

## Hoisting the mainsail

The principle of hoisting the mainsail is simple:

◆ You attach the mainsail halyard to the head of the sail.
◆ You then pull on the halyard to haul the sail up the mast.

The sail must be free of all lines and obstructions in order to go up. In particular, the reefing lines need to be slack.

The yacht needs to be roughly head-to-wind when the mainsail is raised, otherwise it will snag on the mast, spreaders and shrouds.

If it gets difficult to haul the sail up, there is probably a reason: it is may be caught on something, or the leech may be tight because the boom can't lift up. Instead of just pulling harder, look for the reason.

### CREW ACTIONS FOR HOISTING THE MAINSAIL

Before going to sea:

◆ Remove the sail cover.
◆ Attach the halyard.

Take up any slack in the halyard so that it doesn't wrap round any obstructions on the mast.

> **✳ Tip**
> It's a good idea to have the mainsail 'ready to go' in case the engine stops unexpectedly. So you normally attach the halyard and remove the sail cover before going to sea; and tidy up after the yacht is secured to a mooring or alongside.

Before hoisting:

◆ Close the main hatch. This is an important step for the safety of the crew working on the mainsail, on deck. If it's left open, crew members could fall a considerable distance through the hatch, and it is particularly hazardous at sea when the yacht is moving.
◆ Remove the sail ties.
◆ Halyard: put a couple of turns round the winch, and open the jammer.
◆ Make sure the kicking strap is loose, so that the boom can rise if it needs to.
◆ Make sure the reefing pennants are slack – undo the jammers and pull line out from the end of the boom to give more slack.
◆ If the sail was reefed the last time it was up, make sure that the cringles are free of the ram's horn at the mast, and the sail ties holding the reefed sail are all removed.

◆ Ease the mainsheet so that the boom is free to rise (now *watch your heads*, because the boom can swing).

The hoist:

◆ Helm steers head to wind (or close-hauled if sailing on the headsail).
◆ One person can pull, or 'sweat', the halyard at the mast: another can pull in the slack round the winch.
◆ Helm: *look up* to check that the sail isn't catching on anything – for example, a batten catching in the shrouds or running backstay, or a tight reefing pennant.

### ✳ Tip

The helmsman is in the best position to check for obstructions – you can see everything, and you're not struggling with the sail.

◆ When the halyard goes tight, winch it further up to give sufficient tension in the luff.
◆ Ease the topping lift. (Watch your heads on the boom! It may swing sideways.)
◆ Tighten the kicking strap.
◆ Sheet in and sail.

After the hoist:

◆ Tidy up – coil the halyard so that it's ready to run if you need to drop the sail quickly.
◆ Leave the topping lift loose but cleated/jammed so that the boom can't drop too far if the sail is lowered.
◆ Trim the sail – eg adjust the sheet, outhaul, halyard tension and kicking strap (the skipper or experienced crew will advise on this).

### Dropping the mainsail

The principle is simple:

◆ The sail is lowered on the halyard (it may need to be pulled to help it down).
◆ The topping lift prevents the boom from dropping down.

As with the hoist, the yacht needs to be pointing approximately head-to-wind, otherwise the slack sail will blow forward and snag on the mast and rigging.

#### CREW ACTIONS FOR DROPPING THE MAINSAIL

Before the drop:

◆ Close the main hatch.
◆ Ease the kicking strap.
◆ Tighten the topping lift.
◆ Get the sail ties ready.

The drop:

◆ Helmsman steers up to wind.
◆ Release the mainsail halyard and control the drop by easing the halyard round the winch.
◆ After a while, free off the halyard completely and make sure it can run.
◆ Crew at the mast pull the sail down.

✳ **Tip**

Unless you have a **lazy-jack** system (or similar) to help flake the sail on the boom, it's probably best to drop the sail onto the deck to one side of the boom, then flake it onto the boom once it's down. This allows the yacht to resume its course more quickly.

After the drop:

◆ Tighten up the mainsheet to keep the boom steady (it will pull against the topping lift).
◆ Flake the sail onto the boom, and secure it with sail ties.
◆ Raise the boom with the topping lift as necessary.

### How to flake the mainsail onto the boom

Individual skippers/yachts may have their own variations on this, but the principle is to fold the sail on top of the boom, so that successive folds of roughly equal length hang down on each side of the boom. The sail is then held in place with sail ties.

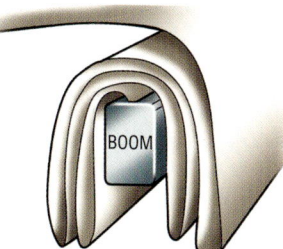

*The mainsail is flaked and tied securely onto the boom.*

**CREW ACTIONS TO FLAKE THE MAINSAIL**

◆ Start with the whole sail on the deck to one side of the boom.

◆ With one person at the mast and the other at the other end of the boom, make a lengthways fold in the sail – tug the sail between you to get rid of kinks and folds (like folding a bed sheet).

◆ Pull the next length of sail over the boom, and make a similar 'flake' of sail on the other side, with a fold at the bottom.

◆ Continue this process – the person at the leech moves forward as the sail gets shorter, and another person moves up behind them and starts putting on sail ties.

When you've finished sailing:

◆ Unclip the halyard and stow it (it clips onto a fixed point so that you can take up the slack).

◆ Put the sail cover on.

**✳ Tip**

As well as keeping the sail tidy (and hiding any untidy flaking), the sail cover protects the sail from ultraviolet light, which can degrade the material. So it's particularly important to use it in strong sunlight.

### Reefing the mainsail

You reef the mainsail when the wind increases. If you have too much sail in a strong wind, the yacht will be difficult to control and will heel over too far.

Sometimes the wind increases quite quickly, so it is important to reef at the first sign of this happening. When you're setting off on a windy day, you can put a reef in before you hoist the mainsail. A typical mainsail has more than one reefing point, allowing you to put in one, two or three reefs for increasingly strong conditions. It's the skipper's job to decide when, and how much, to reef.

The principle of reefing is to produce a smaller sail, by:

◆ Lowering the sail a short way on the halyard.
◆ Attaching a cringle on the luff to a hook at the mast (called the **ram's horn** because of its shape), to form a 'new' tack.
◆ Pulling a cringle on the leech down to the boom, to form a 'new' clew.

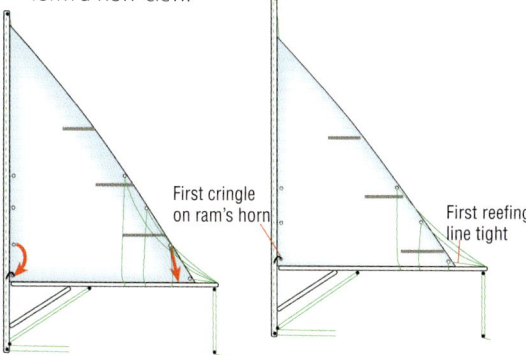

First cringle on ram's horn

First reefing line tight

As with hoisting and dropping the mainsail, reefing is best done with the yacht heading reasonably close to the wind. You can usually do it while sailing close hauled with the headsail.

# Reefing the mainsail

## CREW ACTIONS FOR REEFING

◆ Ease the mainsheet.
◆ Helmsman steers up to windward until the mainsail flaps.
◆ Trim the headsail, to keep the yacht sailing.
◆ Release the kicking strap so that the boom can lift.
◆ One person stands at the mast, ready to haul down at the luff and secure the luff cringle (it's a good idea to clip yourself on).
◆ Release the halyard, and control it on the winch to lower the sail by the right amount.
◆ Pull in the slack on the reefing line as the sail comes down.
◆ The crew at the mast secures the cringle on the ram's horn, and calls 'Made!' to the cockpit team.
◆ Winch up the tension on the halyard (this will keep the cringle on the ram's horn).
◆ Winch the reefing line in tightly, and secure it.
◆ Sheet the sail in.
◆ Tension up the kicking strap.

The mainsail is back in operation, and the vessel can resume its course. To tidy up:

◆ Tie a strong sail tie through the leech cringle and round the boom, to secure it in case the reefing pennant fails.
◆ Use sail ties through the remaining reefing points and round the boom, to tidy up the loose sail.

If the yacht has a **single-line reefing system**, this pulls down and secures both the leech and luff cringles with a single line running back to the cockpit, so there is no need to go to the mast and no need to secure the cringle to the ram's horn. Apart from that, the crew actions are the same.

### Shaking out a reef

When the wind drops, you may need a larger sail again. The reef needs to be released, and the sail hoisted up again.

### CREW ACTIONS FOR SHAKING OUT A REEF

◆ Helmsman steers close-hauled.
◆ Trim the headsail.
◆ Untie the sail ties.
◆ Release the kicking strap.
◆ Ease the mainsheet until the sail flaps.
◆ Slacken the halyard to allow the luff clew to be released.
◆ At the mast, unhook the cringle from the ram's horn.
◆ Release the reefing line. It may help if line is now pulled from end of the boom by hand, to give enough slack for the sail to go up.
◆ Haul up on the halyard until the sail is fully up and the luff tensioned.
◆ Make sure there is enough slack on the topping lift.
◆ Sheet in.
◆ Take up on the kicking strap.

#### ✴ Tip

Don't be in too much of a hurry to shake out the reef when the wind drops: it has a nasty habit of getting up again as soon as you put up more sail. Good advice is: 'The time to reef is when you first think of it. Before shaking out a reef, have a cup of tea.'

## The headsail

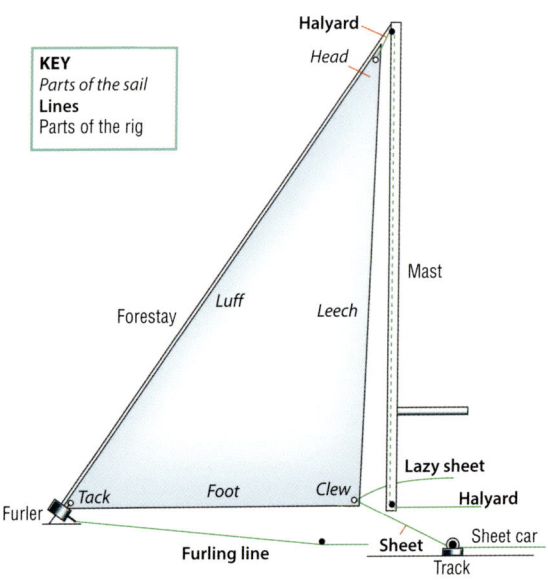

**KEY**
*Parts of the sail*
**Lines**
Parts of the rig

Halyard

Head

Mast

Forestay

*Luff*

*Leech*

Lazy sheet

Halyard

Furler

*Tack*

*Foot*

*Clew*

Sheet car

Sheet

Track

**Furling line**

From the crew's perspective, headsails come in two types:

◆ A **roller furling** headsail, which is found on most cruising yachts.
◆ Several sails of different sizes, carried by some traditional and/or racing yachts.

The advantage of a furling headsail is its ease of adjustment – you can always have exactly the right size of sail.

The disadvantage is that the sail may be the right size but it's not always the best shape, and the thick roll on the forestay disrupts the airflow onto the luff. This is why racing yachts use different sized sails for different conditions, and use the complete sail with no furling.

### Roller furling headsail

The sail is hoisted with a halyard, but usually only once per season. When not in use, the sail is stored rolled, or **furled,** tightly round the forestay.

The sail is normally a medium sized genoa – number 2.

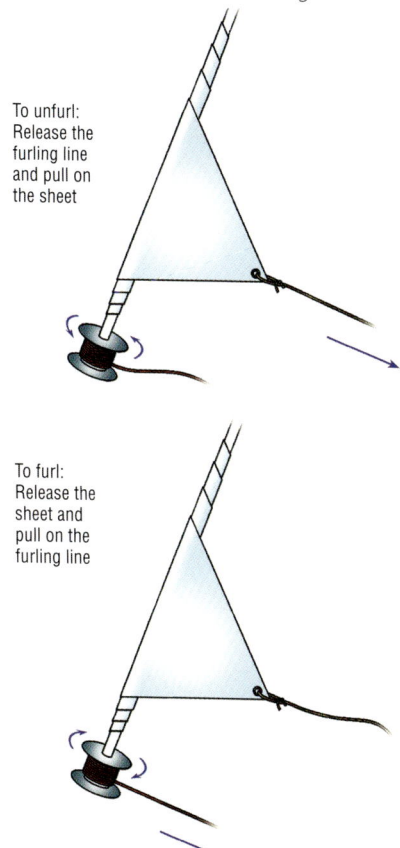

To unfurl:
Release the
furling line
and pull on
the sheet

To furl:
Release the
sheet and
pull on the
furling line

# Roller furling headsail

### *Unfurling the headsail*

To get the sail out, you release the furling line and pull on the sail with the working sheet. It will unroll like a roller blind.

In light conditions you unfurl the full sail. In stronger winds you only unfurl part of it. You use the furling line to control how much sail is let out.

Unlike the mainsail, the yacht does not have to be head-to-wind to furl or unfurl the headsail.

## CREW ACTIONS TO UNFURL

◆ The skipper decides whether the full sail, or part of it, is needed.
◆ Position both sheet-lead cars for the size of sail to be unfurled: the cars are positioned further forward for a smaller sail.
◆ Make sure the lazy sheet is free.
◆ Put two turns of the working sheet round the winch.
◆ Release the furling line.
◆ Pull on the working sheet – the sail will unfurl.
◆ As it runs out, control the furling line on a cleat or winch, to allow the desired amount of sail to unfurl.
◆ Secure the furling line with the jammer or cleat.
◆ Put an extra turn round the sheet winch, and use the winch handle to sheet in and trim the sail.

### ✳ Tip

In practice, the furling line needs to be completely slack to begin with, to allow the sail to start unfurling when the sheet is pulled. As soon as there is a bit of sail out, however, the wind will start to pull it off the roll. At this stage you need to have the furling line round a cleat or winch to control it.

## *Furling the headsail*

You furl the sail by pulling on the furling line. The sheet needs to be slack enough to allow the furling line to be pulled in. However you don't want the sail to flap too much, or for too long, or it could damage itself.

◆ For a relatively small sail, the line can be pulled in by hand. If you ease the sheet *completely* so that the sail flaps, you can then get the sail in very quickly, by hand, to stop the flogging. Get in a good position for a direct, quick haul.

◆ Alternatively, with a larger sail, it may be better to control the sail a bit with the sheet, to stop it flogging too badly. In that case you may need to winch the furling line – which is a slower process.

### ✳ Tip

On a large yacht, be very careful of a flogging sail – the sheets are heavy enough to injure someone who gets in the way.

### CREW ACTIONS TO FURL

◆ Get ready to haul in the furling line – it may help if you put a turn round a winch.

◆ Ease the working sheet until the sail is slack.

◆ Haul in the furling line by hand or on the winch.

◆ As the sail gets smaller, you can control it with the sheet so that it rolls neatly. If there is a lot of slack in the sail it tends to furl untidily.

◆ Allow a turn of the sheets to go round the roll (this means sail won't pull out when the roll is tightened), then secure the furling line.

◆ Take up the slack in the sheets and secure them on their winches.

# Roller furling headsail

### *Reefing and unreefing the headsail*

To reduce the size of the headsail when the wind gets up, you simply roll part of it away. This can be repeated as often as necessary. When the wind eases, the sail can be unrolled again. This can be done on any point of sail.

## CREW ACTIONS TO REEF

- ◆ Get ready to pull in, and control, the furling line – eg round a winch.
- ◆ Release the working sheet so that the sail is slack.
- ◆ Ideally, at this stage, the sheet lead car is moved forward to accommodate the smaller sail. However this can be difficult, and is often omitted or done later.

### ✳ Tip

It is difficult to adjust the position of the sheet lead car on a working sheet. If you are beating upwind, you can move the lazy sheet car first; then the other one can be moved after the tack.

- ◆ Pull in the furling line until enough sail is furled away, and then secure it.
- ◆ Sheet in and trim the sail.

If part of the sail is already furled and you need to reef further, be very careful not to let any sail out with the furling line when preparing to roll more sail away. Don't release the furling line until you are sure that it is slack enough to pull in.

*Crew are pulling the clew line down to reef the mainsail.*

## ✳ Tip

If the furling line is made off on a cleat, you can take hold of the furling line between the cleat and the first block, and haul from there. That way it's always secure, and you aren't in any danger of letting more sail out. Take it off the cleat once you've got some line – and sail – in, and it's not pulling so hard.

### CREW ACTIONS TO UNREEF

◆ Ease the furling line until the right amount of sail has been let out.

◆ Sheet the sail in.

The same points apply about moving the sheet lead car. Ideally the sheet lead car is moved aft to accommodate the larger sail, but this is often omitted or done later, eg on the other tack.

# Conventional headsails

## *Conventional headsails*

Yachts with conventional, different sized headsails will normally carry some or all of the following – listed in order of decreasing size:

◆ Number 1 genoa
◆ Number 2 genoa
◆ Number 3 genoa
◆ Number 1 jib (working jib)
◆ Number 2 jib
◆ Storm jib

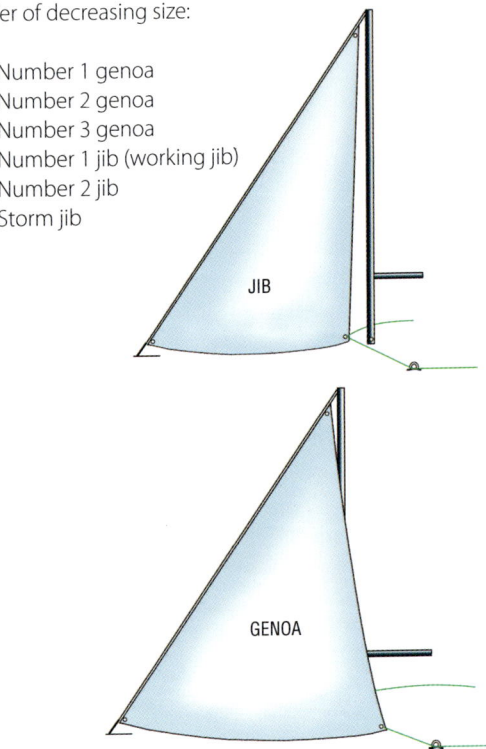

A **genoa** is a sail that is big enough to reach back past the mast. A **jib** is smaller, with a shorter foot, so the clew doesn't reach the mast.

Each sail bag is labelled, so you can find the sail you need and bring it on deck.

## Conventional headsails

There are two ways attaching sails to the forestay:

◆ If there is a **foil** on the forestay, a bolt-rope sewn into the luff of the sail is fed into one of the grooves in the foil.
◆ With a simple wire forestay, there are **hanks** attached to the sail. You clip these onto the forestay.

These sails cannot be reefed. When the wind increases, you drop the larger sail and haul a smaller one up in its place.

You don't need to be head-to-wind to hoist or drop the headsail. However, it is easier to control a large sail if it is not blowing out over the water, so it may be preferable to hoist/drop with the wind forward of the beam. Or for the drop, you can tack without releasing the headsail sheet, so that the sail is backed – then it will drop onto the deck.

*The yacht is sailing in fresh conditions, with a small jib and reefed mainsail.*

## Conventional headsails

### Hoisting a headsail

The skipper will decide which sail they want to hoist, depending on the conditions.

The sail is brought on deck, unfolded, and the halyard and sheets are attached to it. Sails with hanks are attached to the wire forestay at this stage.

The sail is hoisted by pulling it up on the halyard. If there is a luff foil, the luff needs to be fed into it while the sail is being hoisted.

### CREW ACTIONS TO HOIST A HEADSAIL

Prior to hoisting:

◆ Bring the sail on deck in its bag. Get it out of the bag, and position the tack at the bottom of the forestay. Unroll it along the deck, on the side where it will be hoisted (which will be the lee side when it is hoisted).

◆ Attach the tack to the fitting at the base of the forestay.

◆ Run the sheets from the cockpit, through the turning blocks and outside all the rigging to the sail's clew. Tie each onto the clew with a bowline (with a short loop and a reasonable tail). Put a stopper knot at the other end of the sheets, in the cockpit.

◆ Attach the halyard to the head of the sail. Make sure there are no twists in the sail by running your hand all the way along the luff and the foot.

◆ If the sail has hanks, attach these to the forestay.

◆ With a foil, it is best *not* to feed the luff into the groove until you are actually ready to hoist.

◆ The sail can be stowed prior to the hoist by tying it to the guardrail with sail ties. Take up any slack on the halyard so it doesn't wrap round any obstructions.

The hoist:

◆ One person gets ready to pull the halyard in the cockpit (one turn round the winch) and (optionally) someone else can pull at the mast.
◆ Untie the sail ties, and make sure the halyard is clear of the forestay and mast.
◆ With a foil, one person needs to be on the foredeck to feed the luff into the luff groove, using the pre-feeder and making sure it continues to feed in cleanly as the sail is hoisted. (With hanks this is unnecessary.)
◆ Haul steadily on the halyard: go at a pace to suit the person at the luff, and stop if there is a problem.
◆ When the sail is up, tension the luff by winching the halyard tight, and secure with the jammer. Stop the sail from flapping by pulling in the sheet.
◆ Sheet in and trim.
◆ Coil the halyard so that it will run freely when the sail is ready to drop.

*Crew are pulling the headsail sheet in light conditions.*

# Conventional headsails

### *Dropping a headsail*

The sail is lowered on the halyard, with the crew pulling it down and controlling it onto the deck as necessary. It may be secured on deck, ready to be used again, or bagged and taken below.

**CREW ACTIONS TO DROP A HEADSAIL**

◆ One crew goes to the bow to haul down at the luff (this may not be necessary with hanks).
◆ Release the halyard.
◆ Another crew hauls down at the leech and controls the sail onto the deck.
◆ When the sail is fully down, laid along the side deck, remove the luff completely from the foil. Hanks can be left on the forestay.
◆ Secure the sail to the guardrail with sail ties.

If the sail is being changed or put away:

◆ Detach the halyard and sheets.
◆ Detach the hanks, if used.
◆ Fold the sail on the side deck (see below).
◆ Bag it and take it below.

### *How to fold a sail*

◆ The foot of the sail is stretched out, with one crewman at the tack/luff end and another at the clew/leech end.
◆ The sail is flaked by pulling reasonable sized folds (about 60cm wide) parallel to the foot. The crew work together and pull any wrinkles out by tensioning the sail between them.
◆ This process continues, with each flake being laid exactly on top of the previous one, with one edge of each flake lying on top of the foot of the sail.

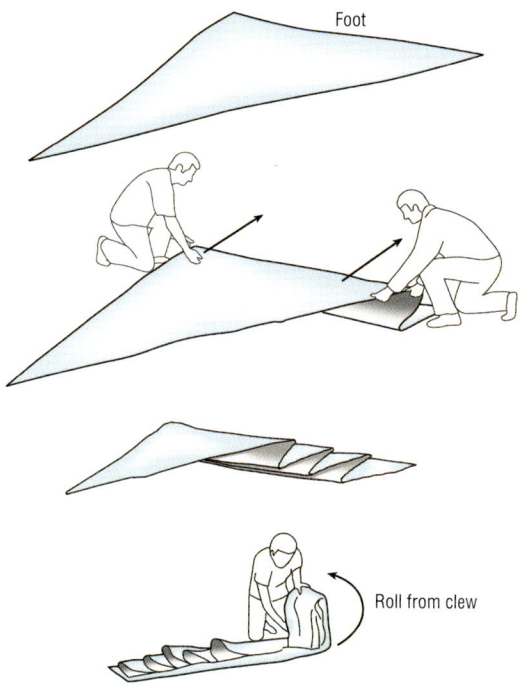

Foot

Roll from clew

◆ As the flakes get shorter, the crew move towards each other on their knees, on top of the previous folds.
◆ When the whole sail is flaked, it is then rolled in approximately 60cm slabs, from the clew end.

The end result is a neat flat roll of sail roughly 60cm², which can be put into the bag.

You will find this easier with the sail laid out on a flat surface like a pontoon. On a side deck you just have to do the best you can – and probably fold the sail again when you get to shore.

## The spinnaker

These large, picturesque sails look ideal for yachts sailing downwind, and they can help yachts to sail considerably faster, particularly in very light winds. They are, however, rather more complex to use. Whereas racing yachts with large crews will invariably fly a spinnaker on the downwind leg, cruising boats use them much more rarely, or use the simpler variation – an asymmetric spinnaker or cruising chute.

This section will describe how a spinnaker is rigged, so that you will know what to expect if the yacht you are crewing on is using one. It's beyond our scope here to describe in detail the crew actions for hoisting, dropping or gybing. There will generally be more experienced crew and the skipper to manage the process and tell you what they want you to do.

### *The spinnaker*

The diagram shows how a spinnaker is rigged. It is hoisted on a **halyard**, above the forestay so that the sail sets outside the headsail. It is symmetrical, so on either end of the sail foot there is a **clew** where a **sheet** or **guy** can be attached.

On the downwind side a sheet, attached to the clew, pulls the sail from the aft end of the yacht, in a similar manner to the other sails. On the upwind side, the corner of the sail is held to windward using a spinnaker pole. The pole is attached to the mast, at about head height, and held in a horizontal position by three lines: the **uphaul** lifts the pole up, a **downhaul** holds it down and forwards towards the bows, and a **guy**, which is attached to the sail at the other clew, pulls it back towards the stern.

The diagram shows only the working lines – the sheet and the guy running through the end of the pole. The sail can be flown on either side of the yacht,

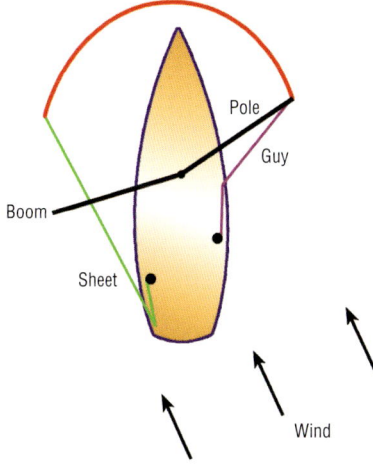

Pole

Guy

Boom

Sheet

Wind

and the racing crew will want to gybe it from one side to the other, so two lines are attached to each clew: a working sheet and lazy guy, and vice versa on the other clew. The sheets, guys and halyard are attached to the

*The yacht is running downwind under spinnaker.*

# The spinnaker

sail while it is still in the bag on the foredeck before the hoist, so you can imagine it is fairly complex and things can go wrong.

> ✳ **Tip**
> One of the dangers of flying a spinnaker is when the wind increases and overpowers the sails. If you have been sailing on a broad reach – the best point of sail for a spinnaker – this can cause the yacht to round up to windward and suddenly you have a huge sail, overloaded and sideways on to the wind, causing the yacht to heel over alarmingly. If the main and spinnaker sheets are eased quickly, the yacht can be steered back downwind. Generally the way to avert more problems when the wind picks up is to release the guy and lazy sheet (the sail will fly out downwind like a flag) and then recover the sail and drop it.

### The hoist

This process involves a full crew, and it's not intended to give detailed instructions here – just outline what happens. Often the skipper will ask an experienced helmsman to steer the yacht (usually close to a dead run, taking care not to gybe) while they manage the hoist and instruct the crew.

The crew take the sail in its bag up to the foredeck and attached it to the guardrail. Then the halyard, sheets and guys are attached without taking the sail out of its bag. The sail is going to be hoisted outside the headsail, so the lines must be run outside the headsail and its sheets. The spinnaker pole is set up at this stage also, and the guy is run through the jaws at the pole end. When the hoist starts one crew hauls the halyard up to the top and the foredeck crew help the sail out of its bag. When the spinnaker is fully hoisted the headsail is rolled away or dropped.

Now the sail is adjusted and trimmed: the pole will be horizontal, roughly in a straight line with the boom. The spinnaker sheet is trimmed continuously: eased in and out so that the edge of the sail just starts to curl inwards.

### The gybe

When the yacht alters course to gybe, the yacht first steers dead downwind so that the spinnaker can be flown on two sheets without the pole. The working guy is taken off the pole, and the pole is moved across to the other side of the boat. The new working guy is run through the pole-end jaws and the pole adjusted into its new position. The yacht is now ready to gybe, the main sheeted hard into the centre as normal and eased out on the new downwind side (see page 51); and the spinnaker crew trim the pole and sheet for the new course.

This is quite a complex manoeuvre, and the exact process depends on which method is used to move the pole across. You can either swing it down below the forestay and round to the other side without detaching it from the mast ('dip-pole' gybe) or, alternatively, the 'end-for-end' gybe where the opposite end of the pole is used for the new working guy.

### The drop

There are various methods for doing this, and in general racing crews will hoist the headsail before the spinnaker is dropped. This should, in fact, make the drop easier because the spinnaker will be shielded from the wind. Generally, the guy is slackened completely (without letting the line go) and the sail recovered (ideally, without going in the water) by pulling the working sheet

## The cruising chute

*Yachts are using cruising chutes on a broad reach.*

and clew onboard to the hatch, easing the halyard and manhandling the sail down below through the main hatch as it comes down.

> ✳ **Tip**
> Make sure no one is using the cooker while this is happening – spinnaker cloth is extremely flammable.

The final job is to pack the spinnaker into its bag so that all three corners are available for attaching sheets, guys and halyard the next time it is hoisted.

### The cruising chute

A simpler version is an asymmetric sail or cruising chute. In this version the tack of the sail is attached to the bows, optionally by an adjustable line, and the sail is sheeted aft in the normal way. This simplifies operations considerably (no pole or guy line) and (in theory) means that less can go wrong.

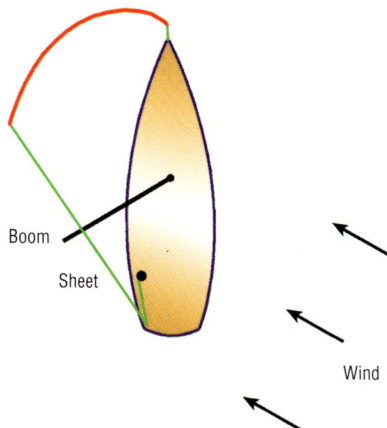

Boom

Sheet

Wind

The cruising chute is used to get more power than the headsail, in light winds. It is not so effective as a spinnaker on a dead run downwind, because it will be blanketed by the main – similar to the headsail. But it will provide good speeds in light winds on a broad reach.

The sail is hoisted in the same way, from its bag on the foredeck. It flies outside the headsail and the forestay, so the halyard and sheets are run outside the headsail. There is no pole, so no need to set one up. The gybe is very much easier than a spinnaker, and easy to do with a small crew. Note that the lazy sheet has to pass round the front of the forestay. (It is sometimes run outside the bows, though this can mean that it slides down and gets caught under the bows if you're not careful.)

It is also dropped and recovered in a similar way. It helps to turn dead downwind for a bit so that the cruising chute is sheltered behind the main and depowered. Some yachts use a 'snuffer' or sock which can be pulled down over the sail, making a manageable tube with the sail inside it.

## Sail shape

Yacht racing is exciting and it can be very enjoyable to be part of a racing crew. Most amateur club racing is done on a handicap basis, so that different types of yacht can race against each other and compete fairly. If you get involved in crewing on a regular basis, you can quite easily be sailing on a 'cruiser-racer' design of yacht that takes part in amateur races.

Although it is for enjoyment, skippers and experienced crew will want to squeeze every possible bit of speed out of the yacht, so more advanced sail trim, and the crew's weight on the yacht, can become quite important. This is good practice also when cruising; if you learn how to get the most out of the sails and pay attention to sail trim, you can reduce your passage time considerably.

The idea is to get the sails to the best possible shape, so as to get as much out of them as possible to power the motion of the yacht. There is a considerable art to this, and this section will simply tell you some of the additional controls and adjustments that can change the sails' shape to suit the conditions. The skipper, or an experienced racing crew, will direct how they want the sails trimmed, depending on the conditions and the adjustments available on the particular yacht.

### *Sail shape*

Shallow camber: strong winds

Deep camber: more power for light winds

A sail is designed to be curved, or cambered, just like an aerofoil. In this way the air flowing over it generates a force perpendicular to the sail which propels the yacht (similarly, with a horizontal aerofoil, you get a vertical lift force).

The shape of the curve is important. A deep camber will generate a greater force and is the best shape for light winds. Conversely, a flatter, shallow aerofoil shape can produce the best effect in stronger winds. With the flatter shape, you can also sail closer to the wind.

Sail trim is primarily about achieving the best shape for each sail to suit the conditions you're sailing in: wind, sea and point of sail. There is a surprising number of different adjustments and controls available for the mainsail and headsail. They can also alter the way the forces on the sails affect weather helm (see page 54). The sections below summarise these briefly, just to give you an idea of their scope and purpose.

### *Mainsail adjustments*

◆ Main sheet: this is the principal adjustment of the mainsail, controlling the angle of the sail to the wind direction. When correctly trimmed, the wind should come onto both sides of the main at the luff (mast) end, which can be seen to lift slightly; at the leech, the wind should leave the sail smoothly from both sides, and the telltales should fly showing that this is happening.

## Mainsail adjustments

◆ Traveller: this affects the angle of the mainsheet pulling on the boom. In light winds, the car can be moved up the track to windward, to allow the boom to rise; and in stronger winds it can be moved down to reduce weather helm.

◆ Boom kicking strap: this prevents the boom from lifting and producing a twist in the sail. It also affects the airflow at the leech of the mainsail.

◆ Main halyard: this adjusts the tension in the luff of the sail, producing folds in the sail if it's too tight or too loose.

◆ Luff tensioner or Cunningham: this tensions the luff by pulling down near the foot, as an alternative to adjusting the halyard tension.

◆ Clew outhaul: this adjusts the curve (camber) of the sail for different wind conditions.

◆ Reefing lines: as well as reducing the sail size for stronger winds, the angle of the reefing lines affects the camber of the reefed sail.

◆ Leech line: this can be tightened to prevent the leech from fluttering.

◆ Backstay: in a yacht with fractional rigging (where the forestay is attached below the top of the mast), tensioning the backstay will bend the mast and cause the sail to flatten for stronger winds.

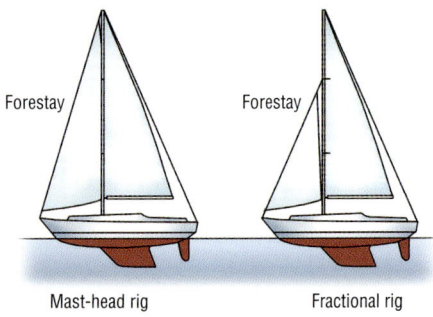

Forestay       Forestay

Mast-head rig       Fractional rig

## Headsail adjustments

◆ Sheet leads: the headsail sheets are run through a block which is adjustable, fore and aft along a track. Its position determines the angle the sheet pulls at, which has a big effect on sail shape. The sheet lead needs to be further aft for a larger sail.

◆ Barber hauler: this is a device that can be used to alter the sheet angle, by pulling on a block which has the sheet running through it. This means the sheet angle can be altered quickly for, say, a different point of sail.

◆ Telltales: these show the air flow over the sail and are the main indicator for adjusting the sheet, or for steering close-hauled to windward.

◆ Halyard: tension needs to be higher in strong winds and looser in light winds to avoid folds forming in the sail.

◆ Forestay: tension can be varied with the backstay, or running backstays for fractionally rigged yachts. The less the luff of the sail sags to leeward, the closer to the wind you can sail.

◆ Leech line: as with the mainsail, this can be tightened to stop the leech from fluttering.

## Crew weight

Sailing yachts are designed to perform at their best when upright, so the weight of the crew can be used to reduce the heel. This is why you see crew sitting along the windward guardrail – in some cases eating and sleeping there during races! This may not be to everybody's taste. Conversely, in very light winds weight is sometimes necessary on the leeward side, to stop the boom swinging inboard and keep the sail shape.

## *Pontoons*

In the UK, floating **pontoons** are one of the commonest methods of berthing yachts. Most marinas have **finger pontoons** for berth holders and visitors: these are small, short pontoons branched off the main one. Many popular rivers have long pontoons for visitors, in midstream or attached to the shore.

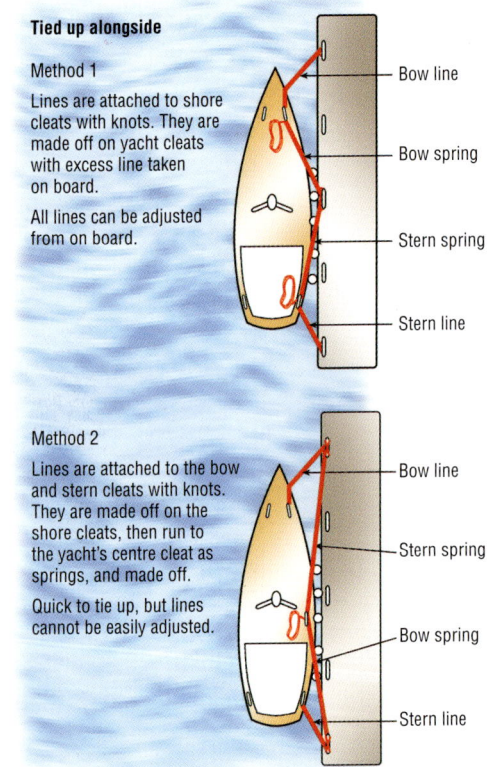

**Tied up alongside**

Method 1

Lines are attached to shore cleats with knots. They are made off on yacht cleats with excess line taken on board.

All lines can be adjusted from on board.

Bow line

Bow spring

Stern spring

Stern line

Method 2

Lines are attached to the bow and stern cleats with knots. They are made off on the shore cleats, then run to the yacht's centre cleat as springs, and made off.

Quick to tie up, but lines cannot be easily adjusted.

Bow line

Stern spring

Bow spring

Stern line

### Arriving at a pontoon

A yacht attaches to a pontoon with **warps**, and is protected from actually touching the pontoon with **fenders**. Before arriving, the crew hang the fenders on the side of the yacht, and get the warps attached so that they can be taken onto the pontoon to hold the yacht.

When the yacht touches onto the pontoon, two people go ashore. They control the yacht by holding the warps round cleats on the pontoon. When the skipper is happy that the yacht is in the right position, the warps are tied or made off to secure the yacht for the duration of its stay, and the fenders are adjusted for height and position along the hull.

The diagram opposite shows the four lines that are required to secure a yacht to a pontoon. In practice, two of the lines may use the same warp, eg the two ends of the same length of rope. The four lines are:

◆ The **bow line**, to hold the yacht's bows in to the pontoon.
◆ The **stern line**, to hold the yacht's stern in.
◆ The **bow spring**, which stops the yacht from moving forward.
◆ The **stern spring**, which stops it from moving aft.

The diagram also shows two alternative ways of using the warps to achieve the same result. The skipper may prefer one arrangement to the other (or something different again), and will brief the crew accordingly.

### CREW ACTIONS FOR ARRIVING

◆ The skipper will tell the crew how they plan to approach, and which side of the yacht will be berthed to the pontoon ('port side to' or 'starboard side to'). This tells you where to put the fenders and set up the lines. Generally the skipper, or an experienced member of crew, will take the helm.

◆ Prepare the fenders. Hang them with clove hitches from the guardrail, low down so that they are level with the pontoon. Arrange them about 0.5–1m apart, along the widest part of the yacht.

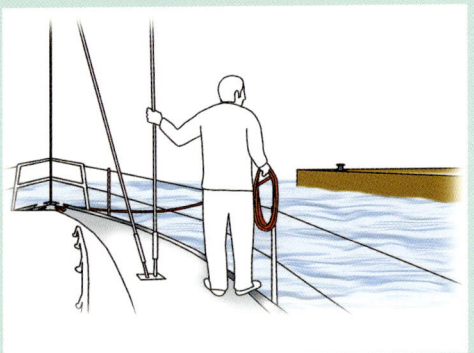

◆ Prepare a bow and stern line. Uncoil a warp, pass the end out through the **fairlead** and pull a good length of warp through. (Make sure that the warp you pass through the fairlead is led *outside* and *back over the top* of the guardrail, so that there will be a direct line from fairlead to shore.) Make the warp fast to the cleat near the fairlead.

**✳ Tip**

Although the warps may be shortened later, it is better to have plenty of line to take ashore, particularly if the wind is pushing the yacht away from the pontoon.

**✳ Tip**

Take care with the length of warp outside the fairlead (which is going to go ashore). Hold it in a loose coil and don't drop it in the water, because it may catch round the propeller if you do.

◆ One person takes the bow line, and one the stern line, coiled in their hands. Both crew stand near the centre of the yacht holding on to the shrouds, ready to step onto the pontoon. As the yacht approaches the pontoon, step carefully over the guardrail onto the toe rail on the outside, still holding onto the shrouds.

◆ When the yacht touches, step onto the pontoon. If the approach goes wrong, the helmsman may decide to go around and try again. Listen out, and don't step ashore if the approach is abandoned.

**✳ Tip**

Although it is a good idea to get onto the pontoon as quickly as you reasonably can, it is probably *not* a good idea to 'jump for it' even if a desperate skipper shouts at you to do so. Both you and the skipper will have bigger problems if you miss your footing and fall into the water.

# Arriving at a pontoon

◆ The crew with the bow and stern lines go straight to a cleat opposite the bow/stern, and take a turn round it to control the line.

✻ **Tip**

There is a tendency for inexperienced crew to try to hold the yacht simply by pulling on the warp. Except in the mildest of conditions *this is just not possible or sensible*: it is *essential* that you take a turn round a cleat in order to hold the yacht, and the quicker you do so the better.

◆ Unless the skipper has asked you to do so, don't 'snub' the yacht to an abrupt halt by making the line off tight on the cleat while the yacht is still moving. Instead, control the line round the cleat, easing it as necessary and taking up any slack, to adjust the position of the yacht.

◆ When the yacht is in position, make the lines fast on the shore cleats.

Once the yacht is secure with the bow and stern lines, you re-arrange the warps to tie the yacht up for the duration of its stay. The skipper will direct the crew to tie the yacht the way they prefer.

The following steps are not the only way of doing the job, but will give you an idea of what may need to be done:

◆ Bow and stern lines: a crew member goes to each onboard cleat, and working with the person onshore they take excess line back onto the yacht. Onshore, tie a suitable knot to secure the end of the warp to the shore cleat.

◆ Springs: you now attach lines from the bows and stern of the yacht, running aft (for the bow spring) and forward (for the stern spring), to cleats on the shore. They can either be separate warps, or use the extra line that has been brought onboard from the bow and stern lines.

◆ Alternatively, attach the springs to a central cleat on the yacht, running forward and aft to cleats on the shore.

◆ Some skippers prefer to make off the bow line and stern line onshore without shortening them, and use the long ends as springs.

◆ Finally, check the fenders. Arrange them in a cluster, close to where the yacht is nearest to the pontoon. Adjust them to the right height for the pontoon, and add a half hitch to each clove hitch to secure them.

✸ **Tip**

If you want to pull in a tight line, it can be easier to **sweat** it. Grab hold of the line some distance from where it is secured (eg some distance from the cleat) and pull the line up towards you – like pulling on a bowstring to fire an arrow. When you let go, quickly pull the slack in round the cleat (two people can work together on this), and then sweat it again.

**Sweating a line**

1. Pull upwards on the line

2. Quickly pull the extra line in round the cleat

### *Leaving a pontoon*

Most of the time, leaving a pontoon is quite simple. The yacht is held with two lines, which can be **slipped** from on board; i.e. they are arranged in a loop so that you can let go of one end and pull the rope in with the other. The skipper is on the helm, and calls 'Slip the bows' and 'Slip the stern'. When the lines are slipped, he motors off.

> ✳ **Tip**
> Make sure that the line will slip cleanly round, or through, the onshore cleat and not get caught. Will it get jammed under another boat's line on the cleat?

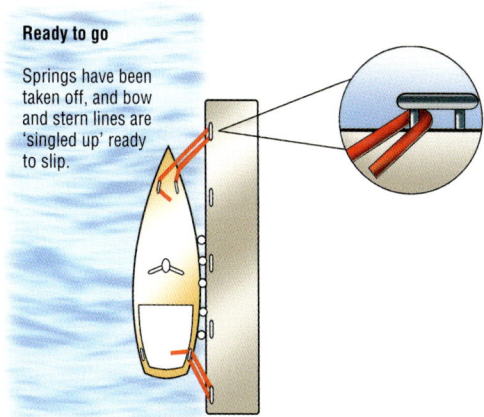

**Ready to go**

Springs have been taken off, and bow and stern lines are 'singled up' ready to slip.

Sometimes, however, it can be awkward to get away from the pontoon – perhaps because of the wind or tide, perhaps because there are other boats in the way. Then the skipper needs to come up with a plan, which may involve setting up different lines and fenders, manoeuvring the yacht in order to turn it, etc.

## Leaving a pontoon

The skipper will explain what he is going to do, and tell each crew member what they need to do.

◆ Make sure you understand what the skipper wants you to do, and are happy that you can do it.

◆ Make sure you know what command to listen for, so that you know when to do it.

◆ The skipper may want to hear back from you when you've done it, eg call 'Slipped!'. Don't forget to do this.

### CREW ACTIONS FOR LEAVING

As explained, there is no fixed sequence of crew actions for leaving. The following are some of the actions which may be needed, and which you may be asked to do for a typical departure.

◆ Set a line up to slip: Also referred to as **single up** the line. This may be the bow line, stern line, one of the springs or a new line set up especially for departure. Onshore, untie the line and/or take it off the cleat and working with someone else on board, pull out additional length line so that you can loop it round (or through) the onshore cleat and pass the end back on board. Secure both ends of the line on board.

**✳ Tip**
If there is a lot of tension in a working line when you are setting it up to slip, it is safer to get another warp and set that up securely as the slip line, *before* removing the original one.

◆ Take off a line: Usually, the skipper will ask for some lines to be taken off altogether, eg the springs, because they are not 'working' (i.e. they're not tight and not important for holding the yacht for the next few minutes). Undo the line from the shore, pull the warp on board, take it off the onboard cleat and coil it (unless the other end is still being used).

**✳ Tip**
If the line is very tight it may in fact be working. Don't be afraid to check with the skipper before untying it – you may have the wrong line, or the skipper may have misjudged something.

◆ Get ready to slip: Undo one end of the line from its cleat, and if necessary shorten it up by pulling on the other end. Keep hold of both ends, and take a turn round the cleat, with both lines, to take the load. Call 'Ready'.

◆ Slip the line: Be sure the skipper is ready before you do this! Take both ends off the cleat, let go of the short end and pull the other to slip. Pull steadily so that the end doesn't flick itself round the onshore cleat. Recover the warp on board quickly, and call 'Slipped!'

◆ Ease the line (without slipping): Sometimes you will be asked to do this. For example the skipper might want the wind to blow the bows out a bit before slipping. Take the ends of the warp off the cleat, and allow it to go completely slack without actually slipping it.

## Leaving a pontoon

> ✳ **Tip**
> In light conditions you sometimes need to 'help' the line go slack by feeding a bit of line out through the fairlead.

◆ Take up the slack/pull in the line: Sometimes the skipper will ask you to pull in on a line – for example, you can pull the bows in to get the stern out. Pull it in, or sweat it.

◆ Hold the tension on the line, then slip: When **springing off** a pontoon, one of the lines will be set up to slip, but will be put under considerable tension first, in order to turn the yacht. Take both ends of the line together, and make off the double line round the cleat (with a full turn and a figure-of-eight) to hold the load. Keep hold of the ends in your hand, and pull on them so the rope doesn't slip. Then, when you get the word, unwrap the line, let go of the short end, and pull the other end in (steadily) to slip the line.

◆ Roving fender: It's often useful for one or more crew to be ready with a fender in their hand, to fend off from the pontoon or other boats.

After leaving:

◆ Remove all the fenders from the guardrail and put them away.

◆ Remove all the warps from the cleats, coil them and stow them away.

## Rafting on other boats

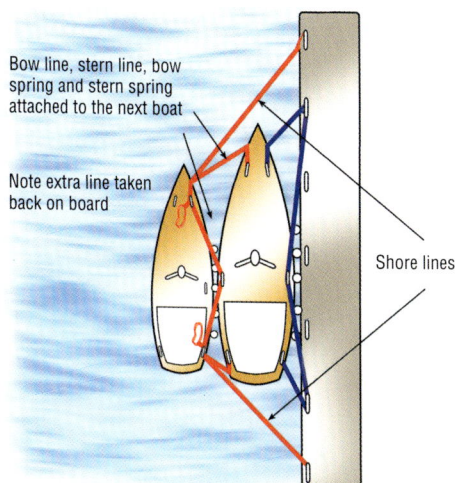

Bow line, stern line, bow spring and stern spring attached to the next boat

Note extra line taken back on board

Shore lines

Sometimes there is no room to tie up directly to the pontoon, and you need to **raft** on another boat and tie up to it. This is very common with visitors' pontoons, where most boats only stay for one night. If it's crowded, the raft may be as many as four or five boats deep.

It may also be necessary to raft on harbour walls or visitors' moorings.

Given the choice, the skipper will normally try to raft against a similar boat (i.e. a yacht) of similar size, which should make attaching the lines easier. The yacht should be positioned so that the two boats' masts and rigging are in no danger of touching each other if they roll.

# Rafting on other boats

As with a pontoon, you need warps and fenders. You hang the fenders higher up, because that is where they are needed, to prevent the two boats from touching. Depending on the shape of the boats, you normally need them right up opposite the toe rail.

The same four lines are used to attach the yacht to another boat:

- ◆ Bow line
- ◆ Stern line
- ◆ Bow spring
- ◆ Stern spring

In addition, you need two **shore lines**; one at the bow and one at the stern. These are long warps that run from the yacht's bow and stern, outside the boat(s) inside you, and attach to a cleat on the pontoon (or shore). They help to take the load, so that the outer boat(s) are not relying totally on the inner one's lines. They also help to keep the raft straight.

*Visiting yachts are rafted together.*

Arriving at, or leaving, the outside of a raft is very similar to a pontoon, and the detail is not repeated here. Leaving the middle of a raft is more complicated.

## CREW ACTIONS FOR ARRIVING

The skipper calls to the other boat out of courtesy, to ask if you can raft with them.

◆ Attach the fenders, high up, with clove hitches for quick adjustment.
◆ Set up a bow line and stern line.
◆ Two crew, one with the bow line and one with the stern line, stand at the centre of the yacht, holding onto the shrouds.
◆ As the yacht approaches the other boat, its crew may offer to take the lines, in which case hand them the bow and stern lines. Be ready to go on board and assist – the other crew may be less experienced than you are.
◆ Alternatively, when the two boats touch, step on board the other boat and take the bow and stern lines to cleats at the bows and stern of the other boat. Bring your line in through their fairlead, and take a turn round the cleat to control your yacht.
◆ Once your yacht is under control, it is best to attach to the other boat's cleat (or other strong point, eg winch) with a simple bowline loop in the end of your warp. On board your yacht, pull in the extra line and secure to a cleat.
◆ Attach bow and stern springs, running aft and forward to cleats on the other boat.
◆ Set up the shore lines.

## Rafting on other boats

### ✳ Tip

Sometimes when tying up alongside another boat, or when leaving, you need to push one boat along the other, or push them apart. If you're doing this, push on something strong like the other boat's shrouds or toe rail. The natural instinct is to push on something close to hand, eg a guardrail or stanchion, but these are not strong enough: stanchions bend!

### ✳ Tip

Remember that this is someone else's boat – someone may even be asleep on board. Ask permission to come on board if there is anyone on deck. Walk quietly on the deck and respect people's privacy in the cockpit and below. Try not to interfere with their lines and deck equipment when attaching your lines, and respect their boat: for example, run your lines through their fairleads.

When crossing their boat to go ashore, walk round the foredeck, not through the cockpit. When coming back (from the pub) keep the noise down and footsteps light.

## CREW ACTIONS TO SET UP SHORE LINES

◆ You need a long warp, or two warps tied together (use a sheet bend – see *Ropes and Knots*).

◆ One person stays on the yacht, at the bows or stern, and another person walks the end of the warp ashore.

◆ The person on the yacht holds the coiled warp and pays it out: the person going ashore just takes the end, and carefully passes it outside everything on the bows or stern of the inner boats on their way ashore (remember to ask politely before you walk through someone else's cockpit).

◆ When you get ashore, you should have a direct line back to your yacht, free of any obstructions on the inner boats.

◆ Tie the line to a shore cleat. At the yacht, pass the end in through the fairlead and secure it on a cleat or winch.

### ✳ Tip

It's sometimes quite difficult to get a direct line from your bows and stern to a suitable attachment onshore: try not to let the line be taken underneath the inner boats' bows or stern, because it may snag.

# Rafting on other boats

### *Allowing an inner boat to leave*

If an inner boat wants to leave – particularly if it's the one next to you – the skipper will discuss what they want to do and tell you what you need to do to help.

## CREW ACTIONS TO ALLOW AN INNER BOAT TO LEAVE

◆ Remove a bow or stern shore line. One person goes ashore to untie it – another pulls it in at the bow or stern, and tidies it up (it may need to be set up again when the other boat has left).

◆ If it's the boat next to you, set up a bow and stern line from your yacht to the next boat on the inside – round your departing neighbour's bows or stern, depending on which way they are leaving.

◆ Untie the bow line, stern line and springs to allow your neighbour to slip out.

◆ Help to fend off with roving fenders (watch your hands between the two boats).

◆ When he's gone, pull your yacht in to the inner boat and set up the lines again. You may need to adjust the position of the fenders.

◆ Set up the shore line again.

## Leaving the raft

If you are on the outside, leaving a raft is similar to leaving a pontoon – see pages 102–6 for details.

If you are in the middle, and need to leave before the boats outside you, the skipper will decide whether to leave forward or astern, and tell the crew what to do.

### CREW ACTIONS FOR LEAVING – FROM THE OUTSIDE

The skipper will plan which lines need to be taken off, and which to set up as slip lines. The neighbouring crew may help by letting go your lines.

◆ Take in the shore lines.
◆ Take off lines that are not working.
◆ Set up two lines to slip.
◆ At the skipper's command, slip the lines (or ask your neighbours to release them) and pull them on board.
◆ It may be necessary to ease or pull in the lines before slipping, to turn the yacht.

### ✳ Tip

When you're setting up lines to slip from another boat, make sure the lines won't jam or snag. They're *not* likely to slip easily if they are run through a tight fairlead and round a cleat with rope on it. Choose somewhere else: you need a reasonably strong point for this temporary attachment, but there won't be a lot of force on it, and it's only for a short while.

## Rafting on other boats

### CREW ACTIONS FOR LEAVING – FROM THE MIDDLE

◆ Take in the shore lines. Go ashore and untie them – pull them on board the yacht and coil them up.

> ✳ **Tip**
> The outer boats will also need to take in their bow or stern shore lines, to let your yacht out. You could offer to undo their lines when you are ashore.

◆ Take the outer boat's lines off (work with the outer boat's crew – these are their lines).
◆ Help to pass lines from the outer boat to the inner boat, round your bows or stern, so they can pull in when you have gone.
◆ Take your bow line, stern line and springs off the inner boat.
◆ Fend off as the yacht motors gently out from the raft. It may be necessary to push the boats apart (don't push on the guardrail – see tip on page 110).

*Yachts are berthed on a harbour wall.*

## *Harbour walls*

Many small harbours do not have marinas, but you can berth a yacht on the wall. Normally there is a special area for visitors, so as to keep clear of working boats.

The same lines are used as for a pontoon:

◆ Bow line
◆ Stern line
◆ Bow spring
◆ Stern spring
◆ Shore lines (if rafted)

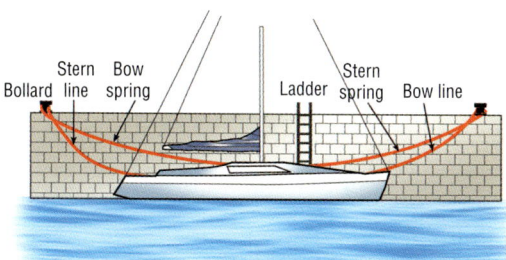

If you are rafting on another boat, the procedure is the same as rafting on a pontoon.

However, if your yacht is tying up against the wall there are important differences:

◆ It is not so easy to get onto a wall – it may involve climbing a ladder.
◆ The lines are not tight because the yacht has to be allowed to rise and fall with the tide.
◆ The lines will probably be attached to large **bollards** or metal rings onshore (unlike the cleats on a pontoon).
◆ It may be harder to protect the yacht from the wall with fenders – particularly if the wall is uneven.

## CREW ACTIONS FOR TYING TO A HARBOUR WALL

The skipper will plan how to get crew ashore, what fenders are needed, and how to tie up. These are the actions that may be involved:

◆ Prepare fenders. For a relatively flat and even wall, hang the fenders from the guardrail at the level where the yacht is widest – normally right up by the toe rail, similar to rafting on another boat.

### ✴ Tip

If the wall is very uneven (eg if it has large wooden piles etc) you may need to tie fenders together to form longer, horizontal fenders, or hang a wooden **fender board** outside the fenders to spread the load. This is not something crew would be expected to be familiar with and the skipper should organise this.

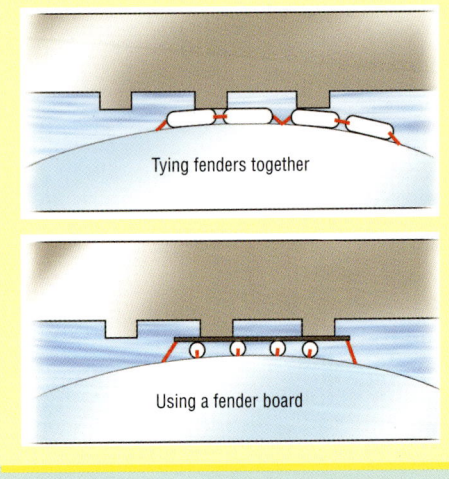

Tying fenders together

Using a fender board

◆ Prepare a bow and stern line as before. These lines need to be very long – use the full length of a long warp.

◆ Two of the crew get ready at the shrouds with the lines. When the yacht touches, climb up the ladder.

> ☀ **Tip**
>
> You can sometimes attach a temporary **breast line** from the centre of the yacht to the ladder, to hold the yacht in while the crew go ashore with the bow and stern lines. It's safer than holding onto the ladder from the yacht.

◆ The crew ashore attach the lines, forward and aft of the yacht, to suitable points onshore. Use a bowline loop (good for a large bollard), or a round turn and two half hitches.

◆ Crew on board take up the slack and adjust the bow and stern lines.

◆ Set up a bow and stern spring – long warps from the bows running aft, and the stern running forward. The onshore crew tie them to something suitable.

The bow line and stern line are not generally attached directly opposite the bows and stern, like on a pontoon. In order to let the yacht rise and fall with the tide, longer lines are used, and are attached to points further forward and further aft. The skipper will tell you how to arrange the lines.

The lines and fenders will probably need to be adjusted so that the yacht sits happily in position against the wall, and can move up or down with the tide.

**✳ Tip**

Long lines are still pulling even when they aren't straight. It is typical for all the warps to be curved when they are holding the yacht in position on a wall.

## CREW ACTIONS FOR LEAVING A WALL

You can't always set up the lines to slip (as you would with a pontoon) because they are too long to single up, and there would be too much friction when you tried to slip them. The skipper will organise what needs to be done. Typically:

◆ You attach a temporary breast line to the ladder, or to a convenient point on the wall, to hold the yacht for a short while. This can be singled up as a slip line, and can be held by hand – while other crew fend off the wall with roving fenders and boathooks (be careful of your hands).

◆ One or two crew go up the ladder and untie the warps. Recover them on board and coil them.

◆ The 'shore party' returns on board. Then you can slip the breast line and manoeuvre away from the wall.

### Swinging moorings

The most common mooring is a single mooring buoy to which you attach the yacht at the bows. This is known as a **swinging mooring** because the yacht can swing round it with the wind and tide. Swinging moorings are frequently provided for visiting yachts in popular areas.

### Picking up a mooring

There are two methods of attaching to swinging moorings:

◆ Some moorings have a small **pick-up buoy** which sits beside the main mooring buoy. You pick this up, pull it on board and attach its rope or chain to the cleat on the bows of your yacht.

◆ Other moorings have a metal loop or shackle on top of the mooring buoy. You pass a warp through this, and attach the warp to the yacht's cleat.

*The yachts are on swinging moorings in a tidal estuary.*

The first type is usually easier – you get hold of the pick-up buoy with a **boathook** to bring it on board. The second type can be harder, because it is difficult to reach the attachment point and get a warp through it.

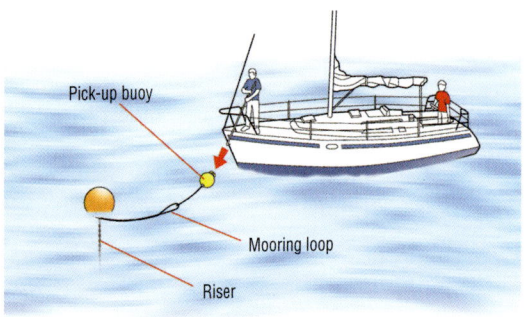

Pick-up buoy

Mooring loop

Riser

### *Clever devices*
There are a few 'special devices' to help with securing to the loop or shackle. Some are designed to hold a shackle (which is attached to a warp) on the end of a pole, so it can be snapped onto the metal loop. Others are designed to pass the warp through the loop, and bring the end back on board. Not every yacht will have one of these, however.

### *Lasso technique*
You can use a warp to get hold of the mooring buoy and pull it close to the yacht. This makes it easier for someone to then reach down, pass the end of the warp through the shackle or loop, and bring it back on board to secure the yacht.

First make a loop with one of the warps that can be dropped over the buoy:

◆ Uncoil a warp (*not* a floating line) and make off one end on a bow cleat.
◆ Measure out about 5–6 metres of rope to make the loop, then secure the warp to a cleat at that point, to form the loop.
◆ Ask the skipper which side they intend to put the mooring buoy when they approach it – port or starboard.
◆ Pass the loop out through the port or starboard fairlead, and bring it back over the top of the guardrail.

> ✳ **Tip**
> The loop should be long enough to throw round the buoy and sink, but not long enough to reach the yacht's propeller.

*Fore-and-aft trot moorings are common in harbours so that yachts don't swing with the wind and tide.*

# Swinging moorings

Get ready to throw the loop:

◆ Stand a few metres aft of the pulpit, up against the guardrail.
◆ Hold the loop with a few small coils in each hand and about a metre of rope between them.

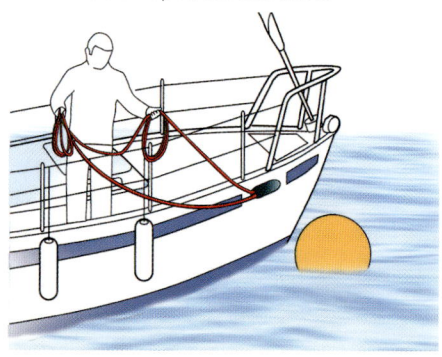

**✳ Tip**
It may help to wet the loop before you use it. Then it will sink more quickly when you throw it over the buoy.

Throwing the loop:

◆ The yacht approaches the buoy.
◆ When the buoy is practically underneath where you are standing, gently throw the loop out and over the buoy. Throw the coils in your two hands *outwards*, to form a wider loop.
◆ If the rope falls round the buoy and sinks, call 'Made!' to tell the skipper/helmsman. If it doesn't, quickly gather in the loop to have another go, and tell the helmsman.

◆ Once it's on, get hold of the two lines at the fairlead and pull them in, to shorten the loop around the buoy.

The buoy can now be pulled towards the yacht to allow someone to reach down and pass the end of a warp through the ring or shackle. Once this line is secured, remove the lasso: undo the short end of the lasso line so it can slip round the buoy, and gently pull it back on board.

> ✳ **Tip**
> Sometimes the lasso line can get trapped under the buoy. Make sure that the line is able to slip round the buoy before letting go of the end.

## CREW ACTIONS TO PICK UP A MOORING

◆ The skipper (or experienced crew member) will normally take the helm, and tell you how they are going to approach the mooring – i.e. with the buoy on the port or starboard bow.

◆ If there is a pick-up buoy, stand by the guardrail near the bows with a boathook. Another crew member gets ready to give you a hand bringing it on board (stand back so the helmsman can see), and have a warp ready in case you need it.

◆ If you are using the lasso technique, get this ready. Get another warp to attach to the mooring, and have the boathook there too, in case you need it.

# Swinging moorings

Don't stand right at the bows – it's not easy to lean over the pulpit to get hold of the pick-up buoy or throw a lasso, and the helmsman can't see the buoy when it gets close. Stand about 2–3 metres aft of the bows to give yourself more room to work. The helmsman can bring the mooring buoy in to where you are standing.

◆ Pick-up buoy: once you have hold of it, bring it in through the pulpit to go over the bow roller, or bring it under the pulpit/guardrail so that the rope/chain can go through the fairlead. Using two people if necessary, get the rope or chain round the yacht's cleat (there may be a loop to put over the cleat).

✳ **Tip**
Don't forget to communicate with the helmsman – a touch of helm or engine can make the job easier.

◆ Lasso: one (or two) crew control the mooring buoy alongside the yacht, while another reaches down to pass the warp through the shackle (possibly lying on their front on the deck).

✳ **Tip**
You can put an extra turn through the shackle to stop the warp from rubbing and chafing on it.

◆ Make off both ends of the warp attaching to the buoy.
◆ Undo the lasso and remove it.

## Leaving a mooring

Leaving a mooring is quite often very simple. Normally, the combination of wind and tide causes the yacht to pull against the mooring on the mooring line – and if you release that line the yacht will drift gently away. Before motoring off, the helmsman needs to be sure that he is clear of the mooring and any ropes etc.

Occasionally it is not that simple – the wind may be pushing against the tide, so that the yacht is pushed onto the mooring. In that case the skipper may need to plan other actions to depart.

### CREW ACTIONS FOR LEAVING

◆ Get ready to slip the line: undo one end of the warp from the cleat, shorten it up if necessary and call 'Ready!' Or get ready to take the pick-up line off the cleat.
◆ When the helmsman gives the order (not before) slip the line by letting go of one end and pulling it through. Or take the pick-up line or chain off the cleat and pass it, with the pick-up buoy, out through the guardrail or pulpit.

### ✳ Tip

If the pick-up buoy is big and awkward, try to get it out through the narrow gap first before letting go the line. You can always use a warp – eg passed through the rope loop, or the shackle on the end of the chain – to hold it while you get organised, particularly if the chain is heavy.

## Swinging moorings

◆ Indicate where the mooring buoy is for the helmsman, so that he can manoeuvre away from it (he won't be able to see it under the bows).

◆ Coil and stow the warps, and put the boathook away.

### Rafting on a mooring

When it's busy, yachts are often rafted together on visitors' moorings. The usual plan is to attach to the neighbouring boat first, and the procedure for this is the same as on a pontoon: see the section on **Rafting on other boats**.

After that, instead of shore lines, you need to attach your own warp to the mooring buoy. This is to share the load with the other boats, and to remain attached if everyone else leaves.

*Yachts are moored fore and aft.*

### Fore-and-aft moorings

With some moorings the yacht is secured at both the bows and stern. The yacht is not allowed to 'swing', but is held in position when the wind or tide changes.

Examples are:

◆ Paired mooring buoys
◆ Pile moorings: bows and stern are attached to large wooden posts
◆ Trot moorings: lines of buoys, sometimes connected with a surface rope
◆ Fore-and-aft berthing to a pontoon or harbour wall (common in the Mediterranean).

### Arriving

You need to get a line attached to both moorings (or piles). Sometimes you attach a long line to one of the moorings, then let it out to manoeuvre to the other.

To pay out a long warp:

◆ Stand where you have room to work, and hold the line in a coil.
◆ Keep the line slack, to allow the yacht to manoeuvre.
◆ Don't let the rope go into the water and foul the propeller.

### Leaving

If the conditions are right, one mooring can be released and you can depart from the other as you do from a swinging mooring (see above).

Alternatively the skipper may have to plan how to get the yacht into the right position to motor away.

## Anchoring a yacht

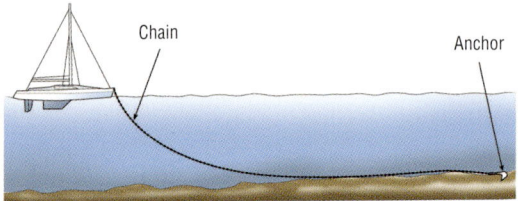

Anchoring gives a yacht the freedom to be independent of marinas and moorings, as well as being useful in an emergency. The skipper will choose a suitable location to anchor. This depends on (among other things) available shelter, the type of bottom, depth, whether there are any obstructions like cables or moorings, and other boats in the locality.

A yacht anchor is quite unlike the classic anchor you see in picture books and pub signs. There are various types, and all of them are designed to dig themselves into sand or mud.

*Anchoring allows you to visit remote locations: Loch Scavaig, Isle of Skye.*

Most yachts' anchors are attached with a chain. The weight of the chain helps the anchor to dig in, and not pull out when in use. Occasionally yachts use a shorter length of anchor chain, followed by a length of warp.

## Setting the anchor

The skipper will work out how much chain to put out, depending on the depth of water and the conditions. The procedure for setting the anchor is to:

◆ Choose a suitable spot, and stop the yacht.
◆ Lower the anchor to the bottom.
◆ Move away from the anchor, letting out the right amount of chain.
◆ Reverse the yacht to set the anchor into the sand or mud.
◆ Check that it is holding.

### CREW ACTIONS FOR ANCHORING

◆ Get the anchor ready on the bow roller.
◆ Measure out the right amount of chain (the skipper will decide how much is needed), and flake it on the deck so that it can run out easily.

Make off the end of the measured length of chain on the cleat, using the same technique as you do with rope.

> ✳ **Tip**
> Most yachts have chain with the length (from the anchor) marked in some way, eg every 5 or 10 metres.

◆ When you get the word from the skipper, lower the anchor steadily to the seabed. Tell the skipper when you feel the weight of the anchor rest on the bottom.

◆ As the yacht moves slowly away from the anchor, pay out the chain from the flakes on the deck (don't just let it go).

◆ When all the chain is out, check that it is attached securely to the cleat.

◆ As the yacht reverses to set the anchor in to the sand or mud, take hold of the chain between the cleat and the bow roller. First you will feel it bump and drag. After a while it should go still, and straighten out from the bow roller as the yacht pulls on it. If the anchor is holding, the chain should feel rock solid and you should see no movement. If the chain bumps and moves, the anchor is dragging. Tell the skipper what's happening.

## Lifting the anchor

When the yacht has been at anchor for a while, the anchor will have dug itself deep into the sand or mud. Pulling on the full length of anchor chain will simply make it dig in deeper, but shortening the chain, so that the pull is upwards, will break the anchor out of the mud.

Although it will be necessary to lift the weight of the anchor, plus the length of chain from the surface to the bottom, the crew should not have to struggle to haul in anchor chain or break the anchor out.

The procedure is:

◆ The yacht motors forward until it is over the anchor. While it's doing this, the crew recover the slack chain.
◆ When the chain goes tight, vertically down to the anchor, cleat it off on the bow cleat.
◆ Small movements of the yacht will break the anchor out, and it will start to drag.
◆ The crew haul it up, and the yacht departs.

### CREW ACTIONS TO LIFT THE ANCHOR

The yacht may have a windlass for the anchor – electric, hydraulic or operated by hand. Alternatively the chain is hauled by hand. The procedure, however, is the same in each case: you don't want to make the windlass struggle any more than you want to struggle if you are doing the work.

It probably works best if two crew members work with the anchor. When hauling by hand, one pulls the chain over the roller, and the other stands behind and manages the chain.

The skipper will be in charge of the helm and engine. They may put someone else on the helm, but they will oversee what is happening.

# Lifting the anchor

Communication between the helm and the foredeck crew is important. Tell each other what is happening, eg which way the chain is going (you can't see that from the cockpit).

◆ The skipper moves the yacht forward.
◆ The foredeck crew take the chain off the cleat, and pull in the slack chain. The chain can be fed into the chain locker; or, if it's easier, pile it on deck and put it away later.
◆ The chain starts to go tight. *Don't try to pull it* – get it round the cleat quickly, and tell the skipper.

## ✳ Tip

If the chain starts to pull hard you will not be able to hold it – it may start slipping through your hands (ouch!) or get away from you completely. Get it round the cleat, or ask your fellow crew on the foredeck to get it round the cleat. If you do this *before* it starts really pulling, you are less likely to hurt your fingers.

◆ At this stage the skipper may decide to move the yacht forward again, and recover a bit more chain. Repeat the procedure: recover the slack chain, and get it round the cleat when it goes tight.

## ✳ Tip

If the chain is marked, you can tell how much is still out. Tell the skipper.

Direct vertical pull on the anchor with small movements of the yacht will break it out of the mud.

◆ Eventually you will have recovered all the slack chain you can, and the amount left out is just a little more than the depth of water. Stop (with the chain on the cleat) and simply wait.

**✳ Tip**

This is the stage when the anchor needs to break out of the mud. If you pull it by hand, however hard, you are unlikely to break it out – you may injure yourself! But if you let the small movements of the yacht do the job, with the chain cleated off, it will break out quite easily and with no effort on your part.

◆ Once the anchor breaks out (the yacht will start to move), pull it up. It will be heavy to begin with but will get progressively lighter as you haul in more of the chain (which is part of the weight).
◆ If there is a lot of mud on the anchor and the last bit of chain, wash it off with a hose if there is one, or a bucket and deck brush.
◆ Stow the anchor and tidy the chain away.

# The dinghy (tender)

### *The dinghy*

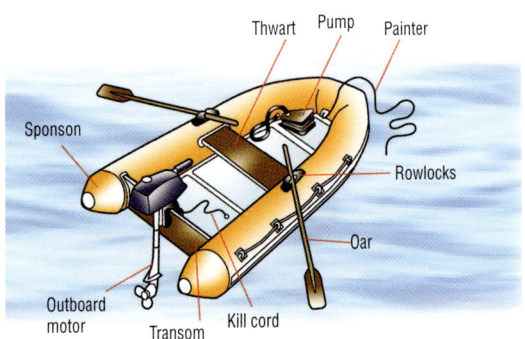

If you anchor, or moor or attach to a visitors' pontoon away from the shore, you will need to get ashore somehow and yachts are generally equipped with a rubber dinghy as a tender.

The dinghy is inflated with a pump on a clear bit of deck, normally the foredeck, or on the pontoon. It's then launched over the side, held with the **painter** (a line attached to the dinghy's bows) and you climb down from the yacht into it. Before going ashore, make sure you take:

◆ The oars (even if you have an outboard).
◆ The air pump (in case you have to top it up).
◆ A bailer or sponge to get rid of water in the bottom of the dinghy.
◆ A torch, if you're planning to be out at night.
◆ Lifejackets, which should be worn from the outset – it is easy to fall in, getting on or off the dinghy.

> ✳ **Tip**
> It's important that dinghies aren't overloaded. Most of them are marked with the safe number of people they can carry, and you might have to make more than one trip ashore.

If you are somewhere with a strong tide, you will need an outboard. Tighten up the clamps which hold it onto the dinghy's transom, and for extra security tie it on with a short rope or sail tie.

Make sure you have enough petrol, and use the 'kill cord' if you are driving.

> ✳ **Tip**
> The safest way to get the outboard onto the dinghy is to lower it down on a piece of rope to someone *sitting or kneeling* in the dinghy. The outboard can then be manoeuvred onto the transom, and fixed on.

*Crew are returning from shore in a dinghy.*

## Crew tasks

### *Crew tasks and watches*

When a yacht is on passage from one port to another, there are a number of routine tasks that the crew will be asked to assist with. They include:

◆ Helming
◆ Keeping a lookout
◆ Sailing tasks (trimming, tacking, gybing, reefing and sail changes – described in the sections on ***Sailing and Sail Handling***)
◆ Taking bearings on landmarks and other vessels
◆ Cooking and preparing hot drinks
◆ Keeping the log
◆ Looking after the yacht, eg pumping the bilge.

On a long passage, the skipper will set **watches**. For example, half the crew may be on watch at 09:00–12:00 and 15:00–18:00; and the other half at 12:00–15:00, 18:00–21:00 etc.

✳ **Tip**

When you are off watch, keep warm and get some rest. What often happens is that everyone is excited and up on deck for the first four or five hours of the passage, then everyone gets cold and tired simultaneously.

### Lookout

◆ Everybody on watch has a responsibility to keep a good lookout, for objects in the water ahead of the yacht, and for other vessels.

◆ When you see something, tell the helmsman and/or the skipper. They may have seen it, but would prefer to be told twice than to be unaware of it. The skipper will decide what to do to avoid other vessels.

◆ Someone needs to sit on the lee side in the cockpit so that they can see under the genoa. This is the only position in the cockpit where you can keep a lookout for vessels in that sector.

◆ Look out for vessels that are working. It is a good habit to keep the binoculars handy to see what other vessels are doing. For example, the yacht needs to keep well clear of:

  ❍ Fishing boats, which can change course and speed abruptly.

  ❍ RIBs or inflatables showing a blue and white flag, who have divers in the water.

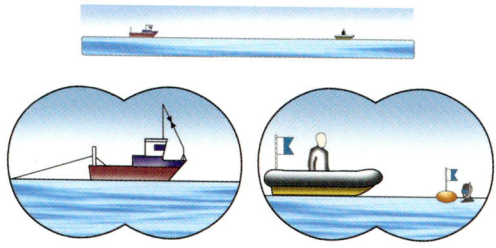

In poor visibility the skipper will organise everybody to keep a good lookout, and listen for fog signals or engines. A crew may be sent to the foredeck for this purpose (remember to clip on and wear a lifejacket).

## Crew tasks

### *Taking bearings*

Another task that may be delegated to the crew is taking bearings with the **hand-bearing compass**.

◆ The navigator may require bearings from several landmarks to fix a position. Make sure you understand which landmark they need, and when the compass steadies call out the bearing clearly (eg 18° is 'zero one eight').

◆ The skipper will need bearings on other vessels to work out if they are on a collision course.

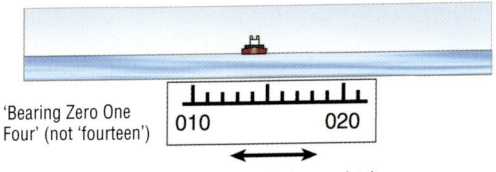

'Bearing Zero One Four' (not 'fourteen')

Unless the yacht is completely steady, the numbers and marks will swing back and forth.

### ☀ Tip

Taking bearings on a moving boat is a skill. Hold the compass level and close to your face (touching your cheek-bone to steady it). Watch how the numbers swing back and forward: you take the bearing by estimating the middle number of the swing.

If you wear glasses, make sure the frames don't affect the compass. Put the compass on a flat surface, let it settle, put your glasses close to it and see if it reacts.

### Helming

As helming can be tiring and requires concentration, the task will be shared among the crew. Remember to:

◆ Keep a good lookout ahead for things like fishing buoys in the water – tell the skipper, and steer to avoid them (watch out for floating rope attached to them).

◆ Keep a good lookout for other vessels – particularly if they are getting closer. Tell the skipper early, so they have plenty of time to decide what to do.

◆ Relax and don't grip the helm too tightly; it will make you tired and stiff quickly.

When you get tired, hand over to someone fresh.

### Cooking and housekeeping

The skipper will plan meals, and you may be asked to help cook meals on passage and clear up afterwards. Most cruising crews also like a more-or-less continuous supply of tea and snacks (biscuits, chocolate bars, fruit, nuts, etc).

Volunteer to help with this, and take care:

◆ The cooker swivels on gimbals, so that it stays level and can still be used when the yacht is heeling over.

◆ Remember the gas routine (turn the gas off after use).

◆ Don't scald yourself with hot water – pour carefully, and don't fill cups to the top. It can be safer to make hot drinks in the sink, so that spillages don't matter.

> ✳ **Tip**
> In rough weather keep your waterproof trousers on when working at the stove. Also, use the cooker harness to support you so you can use both hands. Get someone else to help: eg to hand plates of food, and hot drinks, up to the cockpit.

## Off watch

### *Keeping the log*

The skipper will normally ask for a log entry to be made, say every hour and when there is a change of course.

Although this is the skipper or navigator's task, the crew can assist. Details to note in the log will include:

◆ Time
◆ Log reading (the distance run through the water)
◆ Position (latitude and longitude from the GPS)
◆ Compass heading
◆ Wind speed and direction
◆ Barometric pressure
◆ Notes (buoys passed, lighthouses sighted etc.).

### *Off-watch*

Try to get some proper rest when off-watch. Anything can happen on a passage – for example the weather can deteriorate, or the wind can change so the passage takes longer than expected. If you expected to be tied up by 8:00pm and then find yourself still at sea at 1:30am, it is a good idea to be rested in order to cope with it.

◆ Take off wet waterproofs.
◆ Put the lee cloth up on your berth.
◆ Lie in your berth and relax.

**✳ Tip**
Sometimes people feel seasick if they go below, but lying down immediately helps. When you get up again, it helps to get out into the cockpit as quickly as possible.

Similarly, when you are on watch, try to respect other people who are trying to get to sleep. There's nothing worse than someone yelling 'DOES ANYBODY WANT ANOTHER CUP OF TEA?' just as you are dozing off!

At the end of the sailing trip, when the yacht is back in its berth, there are a number of tasks that need to be done to leave the yacht in good order, ready for the next trip.

The skipper is in charge of what they want done, and how they want the boat to be left. How much you do may depend on how much of a hurry everyone is in to get home, but it is fairest to everyone if you each do your share.

### ✳ Tip
This is where you are helping out your skipper. You may be tired – or thirsty – but you will be much more popular with the skipper if you stay to help with this. Many hands make light work, and you are much more likely to be asked back again.

### *Typical end-of-trip tasks*
On deck:

◆ Reflake the mainsail if it was done in a hurry, and put the sailcover on. Remove and secure the halyard.

◆ Wash down the deck with the deck brush and fresh water hose from the pontoon. Spray the water over the topsides and metal fittings (furling gear, etc), to get the salt off.

◆ If there are bagged headsails that have been used, get them out of their bags on the pontoon, and fold them neatly. Stow them in their locker, or where they can air.

◆ Remove the bunk cushions, brush off any bits and let them air on the deck if it's sunny (and not too windy).

◆ Top up the water tanks (see section on **Living on a yacht**).

◆ Plug in the shore power lead.

## Below deck tasks

- ◆ Make sure the furling line and headsail sheets are secure and tidy – so that the headsail can't come unfurled and damage itself.
- ◆ Tighten the mainsail sheet against the topping lift, and tie it so that it can't come loose from the jammer.
- ◆ On some yachts the halyards are secured away from the mast, so that they don't clatter when the wind blows.
- ◆ Secure the helm with the rudder central.
- ◆ Make sure the shore lines and fenders are correctly adjusted and secure.
- ◆ Repair the ends of any lines etc that may have become frayed.
- ◆ Tidy the cockpit lockers. Put winch handles and engine key below.
- ◆ Bring empty gas bottles ashore.

Down below:

- ◆ Get your own gear packed up first. Once the bags are off the boat, it is much easier to clean the yacht. One person can get a trolley, so that personal gear can be loaded up and taken to the car park.
- ◆ Bag up the rubbish and take it to the marina skip.
- ◆ Take the fresh food out of the fridge or cold storage box, and bag it up to go ashore.
- ◆ Clean the galley, cooker and food storage area thoroughly. Leave the fridge or cold storage box open, so that it can air. Check that mugs, plates etc have been washed properly and are put away tidily.
- ◆ Clean the heads thoroughly – use the toilet cleaner that the skipper recommends (bleach can damage the pump).

**Tip**
The skipper may have a system for keeping cleaning
cloths for the galley and heads separate – coloured
cloths etc. Hygiene is important: what if the whole
crew succumbed to a dose of gastroenteritis when
at sea?

◆ Clean the floors with a damp mop or sponge.
◆ Ask the skipper if they want any hatches left open –
   otherwise check that they are closed.
◆ Close any seacocks that the skipper wants closed.
◆ Tidy and stow lifelines, harnesses and lifejackets.
◆ Sort and tidy storage lockers.
◆ Don't forget to ask the skipper to sign your log book.

While you are tidying up, let the skipper know if you
notice any damage or things missing. Most skippers
keep a list of things that need to be repaired or replaced.

**Tip**
This is often a very good time to ask what things
are used for – if you find equipment that you don't
recognise when you're tidying up.

### Safety briefing

Shortly after you join a yacht as crew, the skipper should give you a safety briefing. The purpose is:

◆ To ensure that everyone understands the dangers and safety routines they need to know about.

◆ To instruct you in the use of personal safety equipment (lifejackets and harnesses), and to issue that equipment to everyone.

◆ To tell you where to find the vessel's safety equipment, and how to use it.

Safety is staying aware of potential dangers. Serious accidents rarely come right out of the blue. More likely they are a series of events that could have been avoided. Keeping the yacht tidy, above and below decks, is a good start.

Typically, the briefing will cover the following topics.

◆ Personal safety
◆ Lifejacket
◆ Safety harness
◆ Gas
◆ Fire
◆ Emergency equipment
◆ Man overboard
◆ VHF Mayday message

### Personal safety

You need to be aware of certain guidelines for keeping yourself safe when the yacht is at sea.

◆ Take care going through the companionway and down the steps. Hold on with both hands, and go down facing the steps.

◆ The boom is dangerous. Take care when standing up in the cockpit – it can move quickly and give you a nasty hit on the head. Generally it is safer to *sit down* in the cockpit, unless you need to stand for helming.

◆ When moving round the boat, hold onto something with one hand, even if you are carrying something. The rule is: 'One hand for yourself and one for the boat.' Get help when trying to move something awkward like a sail bag.

◆ If you see someone struggling, or hurt, it is your responsibility to help (or tell the skipper).

Every crew member should be given a **lifejacket** and **safety harness**. These may be separate, or may be combined in one piece of equipment. It is important that:

◆ They fit you properly.

◆ You can find them, and put them on quickly, when needed.

Take time to familiarise yourself with this equipment, adjust it to fit, and stow it with your own gear.

*Lifeline can be clipped to a jackstay for walking along the side deck.*

## Safety briefing

### *Lifejacket*

Opposite is a diagram showing a typical lifejacket. When you are given it:

◆ Check for no obvious damage.
◆ Check how to operate the inflation mechanism – and whether the lifejacket inflates automatically in the water.

### ✴ Tip

When you are given a lifejacket it is wise for you or the skipper to check the inflation bottle. To do this, unscrew the bottle; check that there is no hole in the seal at the top; then replace it carefully, making sure that it is screwed up tightly.

Fit the lifejacket on over your outer layer (eg waterproofs) and adjust the straps for a snug fit. Check that the crutch strap fastens.

*A crew member works on deck with lifeline attached.*

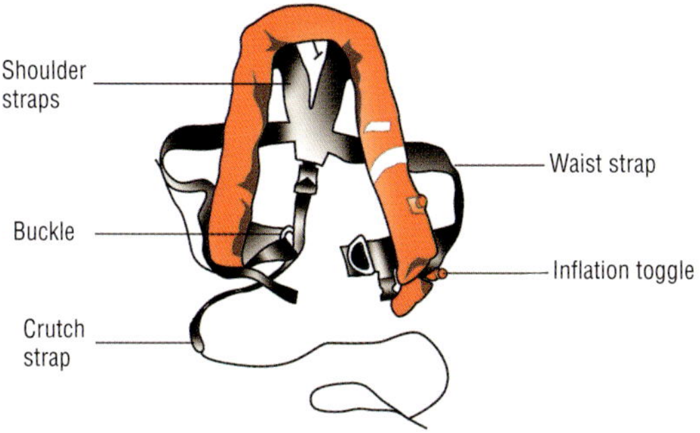

Shoulder straps

Waist strap

Buckle

Inflation toggle

Crutch strap

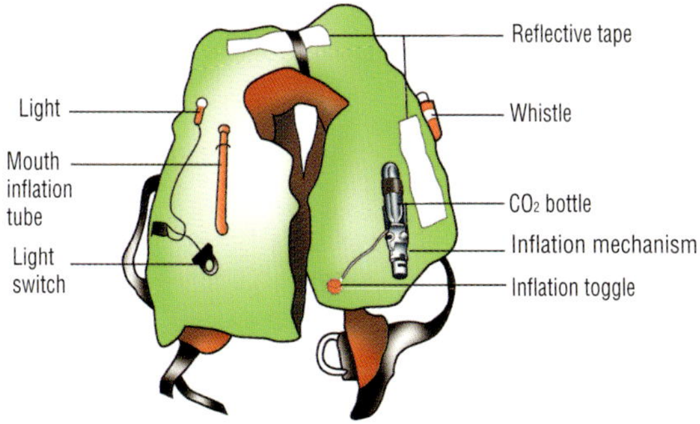

Reflective tape

Light

Whistle

Mouth inflation tube

$CO_2$ bottle

Inflation mechanism

Light switch

Inflation toggle

## Inflation mechanism

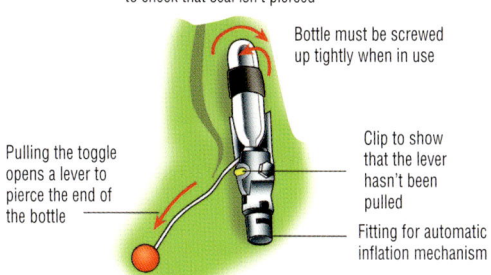

$CO_2$ bottle can be unscrewed to check that seal isn't pierced

Bottle must be screwed up tightly when in use

Pulling the toggle opens a lever to pierce the end of the bottle

Clip to show that the lever hasn't been pulled

Fitting for automatic inflation mechanism

## Safety briefing

### Safety harness

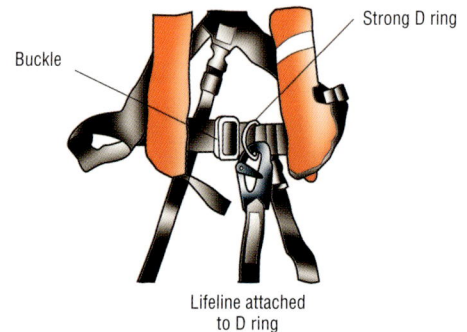

Buckle

Strong D ring

Lifeline attached
to D ring

This may be combined with the lifejacket, or may be separate. Adjust the straps for a snug fit over your outer layer of clothing.

The harness needs a **lifeline** to attach it (and you) to the boat. This may be permanently attached to the harness, or you may be given one (if so, attach it to your harness) or you will be shown where they are stowed.

There are certain strong points on the vessel to which it is safe to attach the lifeline.

### Safe
◆ Wire or webbing **jackstays** on deck (there may also be jackstays in the cockpit) to allow you to clip on and move around the deck.
◆ Strong bracket(s) in the cockpit area – which the skipper can point out.

### Unsafe
◆ The binnacle
◆ The guardrail

Attaching to something that is not, itself, attached securely to the boat may not prevent you from falling overboard – and you may go into the water with something very heavy attached to you!

**SAFE**

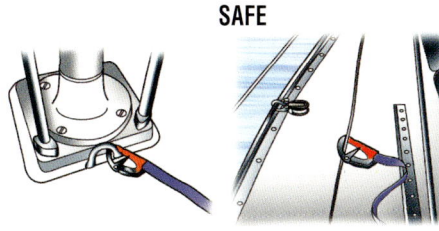

**NO!**

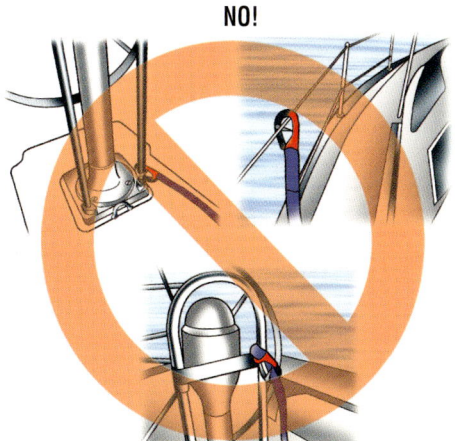

✳ **Tip**

In rough conditions, don't unclip your harness as you go down below until you are safely there. Don't come out on deck without first clipping on.

## Safety briefing

### *When to wear your lifejacket*

Your skipper will tell you this as part of the briefing. Generally:

◆ For non-swimmers, all the time you are in the cockpit or on deck.
◆ Whenever YOU want to.
◆ Whenever the skipper (or experienced crew) tells you to.
◆ Whenever there is an increased risk of falling into the water, eg boarding and using the dinghy, when you can't clip on.
◆ In rough weather.
◆ At night.
◆ In fog.
◆ Abandoning ship to another vessel or the liferaft.

In some countries it is mandatory to wear a lifejacket on deck. Harnesses are not mandatory, but they can be just as important: it is preferable to *prevent* yourself going into the water by clipping on.

### *When to wear your harness and clip on*

Again, this will be part of the skipper's briefing. Typically:

◆ Whenever YOU want to or the skipper instructs you to.
◆ In rough weather – particularly when working on deck.
◆ Sailing in fog or at night (when it would be particularly difficult to find a man overboard).
◆ Whenever you are alone on deck at sea.

The skipper will show you how to clip on when you come on deck. For example, you can hand the end of your lifeline to someone in the cockpit, so that you can be clipped on before you come up the companionway.

## Gas

Gas is commonly used for cooking on yachts. The danger of gas is that:

◆ Leaked gas is heavier than air and therefore *cannot disperse* on a vessel (as it can in a house). It will sink to the bottom of the vessel and remain there.
◆ Leaked gas is a very serious explosion risk.

For this reason vessels tend to have a **gas routine** which needs to be understood by all the crew. Generally:

◆ Turn on the gas immediately prior to using it (at the bottle or dedicated gas tap close to the bottle).
◆ Light the stove carefully with minimum escape of gas (you may need to push the cooker controls in to override the **flameguard** cutout).
◆ Turn the gas off again immediately after use.

If you smell gas, or if the gas alarm sounds, *tell the skipper.*

◆ Turn off the cooker and gas bottle.
◆ Don't make a spark by switching anything electrical on or off.
◆ Pump the bilge with the hand pump.

## Safety briefing

### *Fire*

Fire risk is not particularly high on a yacht, but is very serious if it occurs – it must be dealt with immediately. Smokers must be aware of the danger of petrol (and beware of throwing cigarette ends into the dinghy tied alongside).

If you see a fire, smell smoke or hear a smoke alarm, tell the skipper immediately.

You will be briefed on:

◆ How to escape from cabins.
◆ Where the fire extinguishers are, and what they should be used for.

Principal fire-fighting equipment:

◆ Fire blanket – use for small fires, cooker fires, also for personal protection when escaping from fire.
◆ Water – use on wood/upholstery only (*not* on liquids or electrical fires).
◆ Foam – can be used on liquids, but not on electric gear or electrical fires.
◆ $CO_2$ – can be used on anything.
◆ Dry powder – can be used on anything.

There may be an automatic fire extinguisher inside the engine compartment. Other actions may be necessary for an engine fire, such as:

◆ Activate the extinguisher, or use a portable one.
◆ Turn off fuel.
◆ Block the air intake.
◆ Close the seacock for cooling water.

The skipper will tell you about this as part of his briefing. You will be told about other emergency equipment on the vessel.

### First Aid/Medical kit

Yachts that sail a long way from a safe haven will carry an extensive medical kit. Other yachts will generally carry a standard First Aid kit, supplemented with painkillers and seasickness tablets.

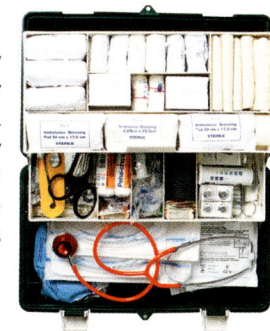

### Bilge pumps

Most yachts are equipped with an electric bilge pump, as well as a manually operated one. They also carry buckets.

### Man Overboard gear

These can be thrown to someone in the water:

◆ **Horseshoe lifebelts** – lifebelts with an opening that can be used by the casualty for floatation.
◆ **Danbuoy** – to mark the casualty's position.
◆ **Throwing line** – a bagged line that can be thrown to someone close to the yacht, to pull them in.

### VHF radio

This is the most effective method of calling for help. Use of the VHF is generally controlled by the skipper, and requires an operator's licence.

You may use it if you need assistance and the skipper is incapacitated.

The VHF is generally left tuned to channel 16, so that you can listen for calls from the coastguard and other vessels, and call for assistance in an emergency.

# Emergency equipment

To call:

◆ Pick up the hand microphone and hold it close to your mouth.

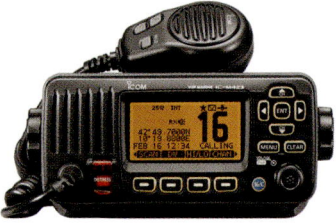

◆ Squeeze the transmit switch on the side of the microphone and talk clearly.
◆ Let go of the transmit switch and wait, to listen for a reply.

In a real emergency, press the red distress button (fitted on DSC radios) and send a MAYDAY message (see below).

The yacht may also carry a hand-held VHF radio. It can be operated from the deck or liferaft.

## Flares

The usual types carried are:

◆ Red parachute (Distress)
◆ Red hand-held (Distress)
◆ Orange smoke (Distress – daytime use)
◆ White hand-held (Collision Avoidance – to attract attention).

Instructions for operating the flare are printed on the flare.

◆ Fire parachute flares downwind, avoiding rigging, and angled away from the vertical if the cloud base is low. Fire them at 2-minute intervals.

◆ Hold hand-held flares at arm's length, downwind and preferably over the water.

◆ Orange smoke flares are thrown into the water, downwind.

Flares are frequently stored in the cockpit, in case below decks is inaccessible.

*Orange smoke is a distress signal for daylight.*

# Emergency equipment

### EPIRB (Emergency Position Indicating Radio Beacon)

This is an automatic radio distress beacon, and is an easy and effective way of issuing a Distress signal. Activate it by following the instructions printed on it.

If you abandon ship to the liferaft, take the yacht's EPIRB with you.

### Liferaft

◆ The liferaft should be thrown/ejected into the water in its bag or case – hold onto the painter (which should be attached to the yacht).

- Pull on the painter to inflate the liferaft.
- Pull the liferaft alongside the yacht with the painter.
- Step into it – wear a lifejacket and put a strong person in first to assist the others.
- Once everyone is in, the skipper can cut the painter with the knife provided.

> ✳ **Tip**
>
> Although the liferaft is very rarely used (with good reason) don't forget that it is available if, for example, you are having difficulty recovering someone from the water in bad conditions. It's quicker to deploy than the dinghy, and very much easier to get someone into than a high-sided yacht.

Generally the only time to abandon ship to the liferaft is when it is *absolutely necessary* – the yacht is sinking or on fire.

A **grab bag** is frequently kept handy, with emergency equipment, food and water. Take it into the liferaft with you.

> ✳ **Tip**
>
> It is very worthwhile to attend a Basic Sea Survival course, where you actually practise getting into a liferaft from the water, in full yachting gear and an inflated lifejacket. It's very hard to imagine how awkward it is to do this, until you have tried it.

# Emergencies

## *Man overboard*

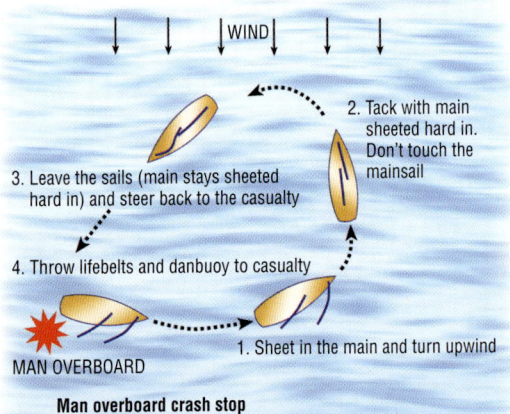

↓ ↓ |WIND| ↓ ↓

2. Tack with main sheeted hard in. Don't touch the mainsail

3. Leave the sails (main stays sheeted hard in) and steer back to the casualty

4. Throw lifebelts and danbuoy to casualty

MAN OVERBOARD

1. Sheet in the main and turn upwind

**Man overboard crash stop**

Subsequently skipper will tell someone to keep an eye on the casualty and will probably start the engine to pick them up

If you see someone fall overboard, *tell the skipper immediately.*

◆ Shout 'MAN OVERBOARD!' to alert the skipper and everyone else on board.

### CREW ACTIONS TO RECOVER A MAN OVERBOARD

The next step is to stop the yacht and go back to the person in the water as quickly as possible. For a **crash stop** the skipper will ask the crew to:

◆ Helm: turn the yacht up through the wind, as if to tack.

◆ One of the crew: will be asked to *watch the person in the water all the time* and point to them. If you are asked to do this, *don't take your eyes off them and don't get distracted.*

- ◆ Mainsheet: haul in hard, until the boom/mainsail is held tightly to the centre of the yacht (get it fully in when the yacht turns through the wind).
- ◆ Don't touch the headsail sheets.
- ◆ Helm: steer back to the person in the water, but don't run into them.

When the yacht is close to the person in the water, it may not be possible to recover them immediately (because the yacht won't stop right by them), but the skipper will ask the crew to:

- ◆ Helm: stay close to the casualty, eg circle round them (without touching the sails).
- ◆ Talk to them and find out if they're hurt: get them to inflate their lifejacket.
- ◆ Throw the horseshoe lifebelts to the casualty, and the danbuoy.
- ◆ Start the engine (making sure the propeller isn't too close to the casualty).

**✴ Tip**

A good skipper will practise the Man Overboard routine with the crew, using a fender (attached to a coiled warp, or bucket) as the MOB.

With the engine started and the mainsail still sheeted hard in, the skipper will steer away downwind and turn back upwind to pick the person up. Crew actions are:

- ◆ *Keep watching and pointing.*
- ◆ Drop or furl the headsail.
- ◆ Get a warp, throwing line, boathook or other special gear from down below, to get hold of the person when the yacht stops alongside them.
- ◆ Help to haul them onto the deck, or into the dinghy, or into the liferaft.

**If the skipper goes overboard, and you have to do something:**

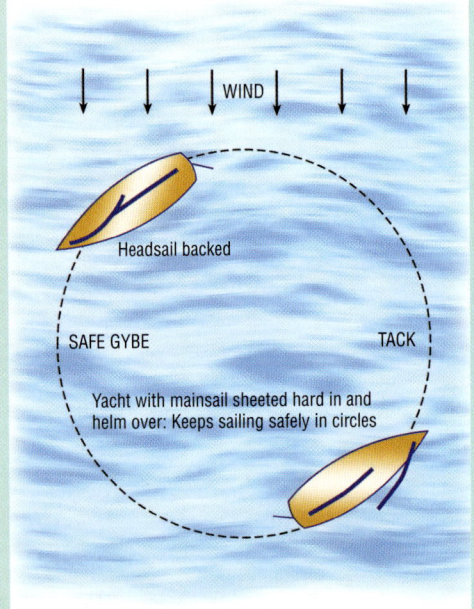

WIND

Headsail backed

SAFE GYBE    TACK

Yacht with mainsail sheeted hard in and helm over: Keeps sailing safely in circles

◆ Steer the yacht up into the wind (as if to tack) and *sheet the mainsail hard in*.
◆ Keep the helm hard over (if necessary tie or clamp the wheel/tiller), and the yacht will continue to sail in small circles.
◆ Drop the stern ladder down, if there is one.
◆ Throw the skipper the horseshoe lifebelt and danbuoy.

◆ Go below and use the VHF radio to call for help.
  ○ Press the red button on the radio if there is one.
  ○ Pick up the mike, squeeze the transmit button on the mike and talk. (The VHF will normally be on channel 16, which is the emergency channel.)
  ○ *Let go* of the transmit button to listen. Someone will ask you what the problem is, and where the yacht is: squeeze the transmit button to answer.

## ✳ Tip

It is a particularly good idea for the crew to practise the man overboard drill (without calling for help), under the skipper's guidance, *before* he falls overboard!

## ✳ Tip

Most inexperienced crew are very much happier to know that, if anything happens to the skipper, there is a simple method by which they can control the yacht and 'stop' (i.e. get it sailing safely in small circles) rather than hurtling out of control towards the shore. That is another reason for practising this early on in the sailing trip.

# Emergencies

### *VHF Mayday message*

◆ 'Mayday Mayday Mayday'
◆ 'This is yacht *name name name*'
◆ 'Mayday'
◆ 'This is yacht *name*'
◆ 'My position is …'
   i.e. **either** *latitude and longitude*: eg '50 31 point 3 north, 04 27 point 6 west' (read this from the GPS) **or** provide *distance and direction* from *a landmark*, eg 'two miles south east of Prawle Point'.
◆ 'I have hit a submerged object/am taking on water/ on fire …'
   i.e. *nature of distress.*
◆ 'I require immediate evacuation for crew/a tow/ immediate assistance …'
   i.e. *assistance required.*
◆ 'The number of people on board is …' (total including everyone).
◆ 'We are a white yacht signalling with red flares/we are abandoning the vessel in the liferaft …'
   i.e. any other relevant *information.*
◆ 'Over' *and release the transmit button.*

Don't panic, speak clearly, and if you miss something the coastguard will ask you for the information they need.

✳ **Tip**
There is an oddly memorable mnemonic for this:

**M I P D A N I O** for:
**M**ayday  **I**dentity  **P**osition  **D**istress  **A**ssistance  **N**umber  **I**nformation  **O**ver

As I explained in the Introduction, the key to learning how to sail a yacht is getting as much sea time as possible. Fortunately, crew tend to be in demand. If you join a sailing club it won't be long before you meet skippers who are looking for crew for this weekend's day out, cruise, race or whatever. Also, sailing schools are in the business of offering weekend sailing trips and welcome crew who may have been with them before. Some want to get additional 'mile-building' experience and skills signed off in their log books; others just want a weekend on the water. In busy yachting areas like the Solent, the yacht clubs organise regular races that provide a good focus for a weekend's sailing.

Once you have gained a bit of crewing experience – with or without doing a formal practical course, like the RYA's Competent Crew – you may want to move on to skippering a yacht, and these are the steps you need to take.

*Skippers need crew for club racing.*

### Theory knowledge

This is what you need to know about navigation, tides, etc. It is easier to learn onshore before applying it for real on a yacht. When you first join a yacht as crew you may be largely unaware of how the skipper knows what to do: although you trust them, much of what they are doing seems a bit of a mystery.

How do you learn the theory? Well, the important thing is the knowledge, so how you acquire it is up to you. There are courses – frequently run as evening classes organised by sailing schools and yacht clubs – or there are books, or websites such as my own, www.aztecsailing.co.uk. You will get a certificate for your log book if you do a course, but that is not particularly important as long as you understand the material.

Here is a summary of the knowledge that yacht skippers need.

### Navigation

This starts with latitude and longitude, which is the basic method of describing position at sea. You learn various ways for finding your position (not just GPS – what happens if you have no battery power?), how to use a compass, the difference between true and magnetic direction and the nautical mile for measuring distance.

*The skipper works out a course on a chart.*

You can estimate the yacht's position by measuring how far you have travelled in a particular direction, using the log, and you learn how to read and plot your position on a chart.

### Tides
A skipper needs to understand tides for two reasons: the depth of water changes (something we're all familiar with, and quite important for a boat) and also because tides cause water in the open sea to move 'over the ground' like a river. Luckily, tidal depths and streams can be predicted, and you learn how to do that.

### Charts and navigation aids
Charts are sea maps which give you an enormous amount of information, whether crossing an ocean, sailing along the coast or entering a harbour. Skippers need to know the symbols used on charts, and to recognise and use navigation buoys, which are marked on the chart and placed at sea to help vessels to navigate safely and avoid dangers.

### Rules of the road
As with driving, we need to know what the rules are when we meet other vessels: which vessel has to change course to keep out of the other's way.

### Weather
Weather has a particular importance at sea primarily because of wind, which can cause dangerous sea conditions, and also visibility: mist or fog can make it difficult to navigate and see other vessels. Weather forecasts are available to seafarers, and you learn how to interpret these.

# Practical skills

### Practical skills

Skippers need quite a wide range of practical skills, and the place to start is generally to do a five-day Day Skipper course, RYA or equivalent. This includes:

◆ Handling and controlling the yacht under engine, including picking up mooring buoys and manoeuvring alongside pontoons in marinas
◆ Pilotage: how to get in to and out of harbours safely, when you might be close to other vessels and dangers
◆ Passage making: how to navigate and manage the yacht on passage from one harbour to another
◆ Sailing the yacht in various wind conditions, and yacht handling under sail without the engine, eg sailing up to mooring buoys
◆ Anchoring: where to anchor and how
◆ Safety precautions and dealing with emergencies.

*An instructor briefs trainee skippers on a practical course.*

Again, the key here, once you have learned the basics, is experience. As you build up sea time you will encounter different situations and conditions, and that's how you learn. It is vital to do this if you want to become a good skipper. Eventually you progress to chartering a yacht with your friends. You can make sure you have a strong crew: include someone who has good experience of helming, or handling the sails, leaving you to concentrate on the charts and navigation.

> ✳ **Tip**
>
> You can take a practical course in, say, the Mediterranean where you are likely to get good weather and easier conditions. But it may be better to do your course in the area where you want to sail. If that's the UK of Ireland, you will need to know what to do in strong tides and poor weather, and it helps if you've done your training course there.

## *Technical skills*

This is probably the most neglected part of sail training. But one day you may want to own your own yacht. As skipper, if anything goes wrong with the boat, the engine or other systems, it's going to be your responsibility to sort it out. Yachts are normally equipped with tools to make basic repairs at sea. You might want to beef up your skills by doing a diesel engine maintenance or electrics course.

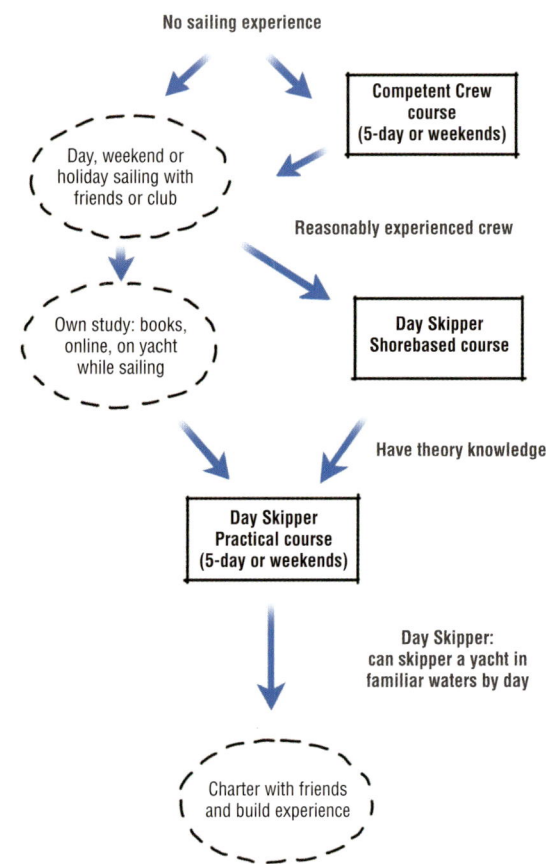

No sailing experience

Day, weekend or holiday sailing with friends or club

Competent Crew course
(5-day or weekends)

Reasonably experienced crew

Own study: books, online, on yacht while sailing

Day Skipper Shorebased course

Have theory knowledge

Day Skipper Practical course
(5-day or weekends)

Day Skipper: can skipper a yacht in familiar waters by day

Charter with friends and build experience

## *Glossary*

**Alternator**  A generator that is driven by the engine to charge the batteries.

**Astern**  Moving astern means going backwards.

**Auxiliary engine**  A yacht's engine.

**Backstay**  The wire stay that runs from the top of the mast to the stern, to support the mast.

**Barber hauler**  Line that pulls the clew of a large sail downwards.

**Batten**  A flexible strip of plastic held in a pocket on the mainsail, to stiffen it.

**Battery isolator switch**  Switch to prevent the battery from being used or discharged.

**Beam**  The widest part of the yacht.

**Beam reach**  Point of sail with the wind on the beam.

**Bear away**  To alter course away from the wind direction.

**Bearing**  The measurement of compass direction to an object.

**Beating**  Sailing to an upwind destination, by tacking.

**Bend**  A type of knot that joins two ropes together.

**Berth  a)** Bed or bunk on board **b)** place for the yacht to lie, eg in a marina.

**Bilge**  Where water gathers on a yacht, under the floorboards.

**Bilge pump**  Pump to remove water from the bilge.

**Binnacle**  Pillar that holds the wheel and steering compass.

**Boathook**  A long handled hook for picking up ropes etc in the water.

**Bollard**  A stone or metal strong point ashore, for tying warps to.

**Bolt rope**  A cord sewn into the edge of a sail to hold the sail in a groove or track.

**Boom**  The horizontal spar from the mast, at the base of the mainsail.

**Bow line**  When alongside, the line which holds the yacht in at the bows.

**Bow spring**  When alongside, the line which stops the yacht from moving forward.

**Bowline**  Knot used to tie a loop in the end of a rope.

**Bows**  The front of the yacht.

**Breast line**  When alongside, a line to the shore from the centre of the yacht.

**Broad reach**  Point of sail with the wind aft of the beam.

**Cleat, Cleat off**  Strong double-ended hook on the deck or pontoon, for attaching warps and other lines to. To secure to a cleat.

**Clew**  The aft corner of a sail, where the sheet attaches.

**Close-hauled**  Point of sail which is as close to the wind as the yacht can sail.

**Clove hitch**  Knot commonly used to attach fenders to a guardrail.

**Companionway**  The passage from the deck to below decks.

**Compass course**  The course that the navigator wants the yacht to steer.

**Controlled gybe**  A gybe in which the boom is controlled (as opposed to an *accidental gybe* which is dangerous).

**Crash stop**  Manoeuvre where the yacht quickly stops and turns back, eg for a man overboard.

**Cringle**  A reinforced hole in the sail for reefing lines etc.

**Danbuoy**  Buoy with a flag that can be dropped overboard to mark the position of a man overboard.

**Dead run**  Point of sail where the wind is directly behind the yacht.

**Domestic battery**  The 12-volt battery(s) used to power onboard lights and other systems.

**Double sheet bend**  Secure knot for joining two ropes.

**Downhaul**  The line which pulls the spinnaker pole downwards.

**Ease**  To slowly or gradually let out a line.

**Engine battery**  The 12-volt battery used to start the engine.

**Engine control**  The control for the engine, with neutral, forward and reverse gears and different engine speeds. (Gear and throttle control.)

**EPIRB**  Stands for Emergency Position Indicating Radio Beacon.

**Fairlead**  Reinforced gap in the toe rail, or upper part of the topsides, for passing a warp through.

**Fender**  Protective 'cushions' to hang from the yacht when alongside, to prevent damage to the topsides.

**Fender board**  Wooden board which hangs outside the fenders.

**Figure-of-eight**  A stopper knot, to prevent sheets or other lines from pulling through a block of jammer.

**Fine reach**  Point of sail with the wind forward of the beam.

**Finger pontoon**  A narrow pontoon in a marina, for yachts to tie alongside.

**Flake**  To arrange a sail (or rope, or chain) in successive folds.

**Flameguard**  Device on a cooker that cuts off the gas if the flame goes out.

**Flares**  Pyrotechnics carried onboard for to signal an emergency or to attract attention.

**Foil**  A metal/plastic extrusion fitted to the forestay to hold the luff of the headsail.

**Foot**  The bottom edge of a sail.

**Forestay**  The wire stay that runs from the mast to the stem of the yacht, to support the mast. Also holds the headsail luff.

**Free off**  To alter course away from the wind, and ease the sheets.

**Furl**  To roll up a sail.

**Furling line**  The line that controls a sail's roller furling equipment.

**Galley**  The area below decks for food storage and preparation.

**Gas routine**  Procedure to be followed when using gas.

**Gear and throttle control**  *See* **Engine control.**

**Generator**  A machine that generates electricity to charge the batteries. It may also provide 240-volt power.

**Genoa**  A large headsail, which extends aft of the mast.

**Grab bag**  A bag containing emergency equipment for abandoning the yacht.

**Guardrail**  The wire 'fence' surrounding the deck.

**Guy**  Line pulling the spinnaker pole aft.

**Gybe**  To turn the stern through the wind, bringing the wind onto the opposite side of the yacht. (*See also* **Controlled Gybe**.)

**Halyard**  Line used to hoist a sail.

**Hand-bearing compass**  A hand-held compass used for taking bearings.

**Hand rail**  The hand holds for going down the side deck.

**Hank(s)**  To attach the headsail to the forestay. Also, the clips that do this.

**Harden up**  To alter course to windward, and sheet in the sails.

**Harness**  Personal safety gear for clipping on to the yacht.

**Hatch**  An opening in the deck. The *main hatch* opens into the companionway to go below.

**Head**  The top corner of a sail (where the halyard attaches).

**Heads**  Onboard toilet and washing area.

**Helm**  The steering position, with wheel or tiller. To steer the yacht.

**Holding tank**  A tank for waste from the heads.

**Horseshoe lifebelt**  A lifebelt with an opening, generally carried on the pushpit for man overboard emergencies.

**In-mast furling**  System for rolling up the mainsail inside the mast.

**Inverter**  Device that provides domestic 240-volt AC power from 12-volt batteries.

**Isolator switch**  *See* **Battery Isolator switch**.

**Jackstay**  A wire or webbing strip to attach a lifeline to.

**Jib**  Small headsail, which doesn't reach beyond the mast.

**Kicking strap**  Line to pull the boom down, to tighten the mainsail leech.

**Lasso**  A loop of warp used to get hold of a mooring buoy.

**Lavac**  Design of heads with a vacuum flush system, that operates by sucking seawater in as the heads is pumped out.

**Lazy sheet**  The headsail sheet that isn't in use.

**Lazy-jack**  An arrangement to help flake the mainsail onto the boom.

**Lee cloth**  Panel of strong cloth used to prevent someone rolling out of a berth.

**Leech**  The back edge of a sail, from the head to the clew.

**Leech line**  A cord that can be tensioned to stop the leech of the sail from fluttering.

**Lifeline**  Used with a harness for attaching to a strong point or jackstay on deck.

**Liferaft**  Used for emergency inflation and evacuation from the yacht.

**Locking turn**  Final turn on a cleat tied so that it goes tight if the line slips.

**Log a)** Instrument for measuring the speed of the yacht and distance run **b)** book for recording navigational and other information.

**Luff**  The leading edge of a sail.

**Luff cunningham**  Line used to tension the luff of a mainsail by pulling it downwards.

**Luff groove**  The groove in the foil to hold the headsail luff.

**Luffing up**  Coming too close to the wind (which slows a yacht down).

**Mainsheet**  *See* **Sheet**.

**Mainsail**  The sail which is hoisted aft of the main mast.

**Mayday**  International distress signal (from the French 'M'aidez').

**Mooring line**  A line attaching the yacht to a mooring.

**Outhaul**  Line that tightens the foot of the mainsail, by pulling the clew outwards to the end of the boom.

**Painter**  A line attached to the bows of a dinghy.

**Pick-up buoy**  A small buoy for picking up a mooring.

**Point of sail**  The direction the yacht is sailing in, with respect to the wind.

**Pontoon**  A floating platform for yachts to berth on.

**Port**  The left-hand side of a boat (looking forwards).

**Port tack**  Sailing with the wind on the port side of the yacht.

**Pre-heat**  Used to heat a diesel engine so that it starts easily.

**Preventer**  A strong line rigged to prevent the mainsail/boom from gybing.

**Prop walk**  The sideways push of a propeller (particularly in reverse).

**Prop wash**  The wash from a propeller (which can push on the rudder).

**Pulpit**  The solid metal frame at the bows (forward of the guardrail).

**Pushpit**  A similar frame to the pulpit, round the aft deck or cockpit, at the stern.

**Rafting**  Berthing alongside another boat.

**Ram's horn**  Hooks at the mast to which you secure a cringle when reefing the mainsail.

**Reef**  To reduce the size of a sail.

**Reef knot**  A knot which can be used to tie up a bundle of sail.

**Reefing lines/pennants**  Lines used to reef the mainsail, by pulling the leech down to the boom (usually there are three – first, second and third).

**Reverse osmosis**  A process for making fresh water from seawater.

**Riding turn**  A turn on a winch which overlaps another turn (and jams it).

**Rig/rigging**  The mast(s), boom and stays – which carry the sails.

**Roller furling**  A system for rolling up a sail – normally the headsail.

**Roller furling line**  *See* **Furling line.**

**Rolling hitch**  A knot similar to a clove hitch, used to grip one line with another.

**Round turn and two half hitches**  A knot used to tie a rope to a strong point, eg to tie up a boat.

**Roving fender**  A fender that is held in the hand and can be used anywhere quickly.

**Rudder**  Pivoting blade that steers the boat.

**Running**  *See* **Dead run.**

**Running backstay**  A backstay that can be tightened or loosened.

**Safety harness**  *See* **Harness.**

**Sail tie**  Short length of line used to secure a bundle of sail.

**Saloon**  'Living area' below decks.

**Seacock**  A valve to shut off a pipe which has access to the sea through the hull.

**Self-tailer**  Part of a winch that grips the line, so effectively tails it.

**Sheet**  The line used to control the clew of a sail (and the boom, in the case of the mainsheet).

**Sheet bend**  A knot for joining two ropes together.

**Sheet car**  A moveable block through which the headsail sheet passes, on its way to the cockpit.

**Shore line**  When berthing alongside another boat, warps that attach the yacht directly to the shore.

**Shore power**  The 240-volt electricity supply from the shore (via a socket on the pontoon).

**Shrouds**  The rigging wires that run from the side of the mast to the side decks, to support the mast.

**Single-line reefing**  A system that pulls down the leech and luff of the mainsail simultaneously, when reefing.

**Single up**  To make a loop of a warp so that it can be slipped from on board.

**Slip**  To release a line which is holding the yacht (to the shore, mooring or other boat) and recover it on board.

**Spinnaker**  A large extra sail for sailing on a broad reach or dead run.

**Spring**  *See* **Bow spring, Stern spring.**

**Spring off**  The manoeuvre to turn the yacht by pulling against a spring with the engine.

**Square-knot**  *See* **Reef knot.**

**Stanchion**  Post that supports the guardrail.

**Starboard**  The right-hand side of a boat (looking forwards).

**Starboard tack**  Sailing with the wind on the starboard side of the yacht.

**Stem**  The very front of the yacht.

**Stern**  The back of the yacht.

**Stern line**  When alongside, the line which holds the yacht in at the stern.

**Stern spring**  When alongside, the line which stops the yacht from moving astern.

**Stop button/lever**  Control to stop the engine.

**Storm jib**  A small, strong headsail for use in very windy conditions.

**Sweat**  To pull a line in by pulling it sideways.

**Swinging mooring**  A mooring that holds a boat at the bows only, allowing it to swing with the wind and tide.

**Tack**  To turn the bows through the wind, bringing the wind onto the opposite side of the yacht.

**Tail  a)** The action of holding a rope under tension so that it grips on a winch **b)** the end of a rope, especially at a knot.

**Telltale**  A small piece of material attached to the sail that shows the flow of the wind over its surface.

**Tender**  Small boat used to get between the yacht and the shore.

**Throwing line**  An emergency line used to throw to someone in the water.

**Tiller**  A long lever attached to the rudder, used to steer the boat.

**Toe rail**  The low rail along the edge of the deck.

**Topping lift**  The line used to support the boom when the mainsail isn't hoisted.

**Topsides**  The side of the yacht's hull above the waterline.

**Transom**  The flat part of the hull at the stern of a boat.

**Trim**  To adjust the sails.

**Uphaul**  The line that supports the spinnaker pole, pulling it upwards.

**Vang**  Strut which supports the boom by pushing upwards from the mast.

**VHF radio**  Standard marine radio communication.

**Warp**  A rope used to tie up or secure a yacht.

**Washboard**  Removable board to close off the main hatch.

**Watch**  System whereby some of the crew rest, while the others look after the yacht.

**Water maker**  Device for making fresh water from sea water.

**Weather helm**  When sailing, the tendency of the yacht to turn up to wind (and the helm needed to counteract that).

**Wheel**  The wheel used to turn the rudder, to steer the boat.

**Winch**  Device for pulling a rope with increased force.

**Winch barrel**  The part of the winch that you wrap the rope round.

**Winch handle**  The handle that fits into the top of the winch to turn it.

**Working**  In use, or under tension (of a warp or sheet).

# Index

INDEX

Auxiliary engine 9, 35–43
Alternator 14
Anchor, anchoring 128–135
– lifting 131–133
– setting 129–130
– windlass 131
Astern, Steering 40–1

Backstay 8, 94
Barber hauler 95
Batten 65
Battery isolator switch 14, 36, 37
Beam reach 46
Bearing 138
Bearing away 47
Beating 56
Bend 33
Berth 9, 16
Berthing 96–118
Bilge 9
Bilge pump 153
Binnacle 8
Boathook 120
Bollard 115
Bolt rope 81
Boom 66–73
Boom kicking strap 94
Bow line 19, 97, 108, 115
Bow spring 19, 97, 108, 115
Bowline 34
Bows 8
Breast line 19, 117
Broad reach 46, 60–63

Charts and navigation aids 165
Cleat 8, 26–27
Clew 65, 74, 87
Clew outhaul 94
Close-hauled 46, 58–59
Clove hitch 30
Coil 20–21
Companionway 8, 9
Compass course 56–57
Crash stop 158–159
Crew weight 95
Cringle 65, 71
Cruising chute 90–92
Cunningham 94

Danbuoy 153
Dead run (sailing downwind) 46, 60–63, 88, 89
Dinghy 134–135
Domestic battery 14
Double sheet bend 33
Downhaul 19, 87
Driving rules 165

Ease 25
Electricity 14–15
End-of-trip 141–143
Engine 35–43
– control 35
– starting and stopping 36–37
Engine battery 14, 36, 37
EPIRB 156

Fairlead 8, 98–99
Fender 8, 97
Fender board 116
Figure-of-eight 28
Fine reach 46
Finger pontoon 96
Fire 152
Flake 69–70, 84–85, 119
Flameguard 151
Flares 154–155
Folding a sail 84–85
Food and cooking 10, 139
Foot 65, 74
Fore-and-aft mooring 127
Forestay 8, 74, 95
Free off 47
Fresh water 11
Furl 75
Furling line 74–79

Galley 9, 10
Gas, gas routine 10, 151
Gear and throttle control 35
Generator 15
Genoa 80–81
Grab bag 157
Guardrail 8
Guy 19, 87
Gybe 51–53

Halyard 18, 65, 74, 87, 94, 95
Hand rail 8
Hand-bearing compass 138
Hank(s) 81
Harbour walls 115–118
– leaving 118
– tying up 115–117
Harden up 47
Harness 145, 148–150
Hatch 8
Head 65, 74
Heads, toilet 9, 12–13
Headsail 74–85, 95
– dropping 84
– hoisting 82–83
Helm, helming (steering) 38–41, 54–61, 139
Holding tank 12
Horseshoe lifebelt 153

Inverter 15
Isolator switch 14, 36, 37

Jackstay 148
Jib 80–81

Kicking strap 18, 65, 94
Knots 28–34

Lasso 120–123
Lavac 12, 13
Lazy-jack 68
Lee cloth 9, 16
Leech 65, 74
Leech line 94, 95
Lifejacket 145–147, 150
Lifeline 148
Liferaft 156–157
Locking turn 27
Log 140
Lookout 137
Luff 65, 74
Luff groove 81
Luff tensioner 94

Mainsail 65–73, 93–94
– dropping 68–69
– flaking 69–70
– hoisting 65–67
– reefing 71–73
Mainsheet 18, 65

# Index

**INDEX**

Man overboard 153, 158–161
Mayday message 162
Mooring 119–127
– fore-and-aft 127
– leaving a mooring 125–126, 127
– rafting on 126
– swinging 119–126
Mooring line 19
Motor 35–43

Navigation 164–165

Outhaul 18, 65, 94

Painter 19, 134
Passage 136–140
Pick-up buoy 119–120
Point of sail 46
Pontoon 96–106
– leaving a pontoon 102–106
Port 8
Port tack 46
Pre-heat 36
Preventer 18, 61–64
Prop walk 42
Prop wash 43
Pulpit 8
Pushpit 8

Racing, advanced trimming and 92–95
– crew weight 95
– headsail adjustments 95
– mainsail adjustments 93–94
– sail shape 92–93
Rafting 107–114, 126
– leaving a raft 112–114
Ram's horn 71
Reef knot 29
Reefing 71–73, 78–79
– single line 72
– shaking out 73
Reefing lines/pennants 18, 65, 71–73, 94
Reverse osmosis water makers 11
Riding turn 23

Roller furling 74–79
Roller furling line 18, 74–79
Rolling hitch 31
Ropes 17–27
Round turn and two half hitches 32
Roving fender 105
Rubbish 15
Rudder 8, 38–39
Running (sailing downwind) 60–63

Safety 144–162
– emergencies 152–162
Safety harness 145, 148–150
Sail tie 19
Sail trim 44–45, 92–95
Sailing downwind 46, 60–63, 88, 89
Saloon 9
Seacock 12, 36, 143
Self-tailing winches 24
Sheet 18, 65, 74, 87
Sheet bend 33
Sheet car 74
Sheet leads 95
Shore power 15
Shoreline 19, 107, 108, 112, 115
Shrouds 8
Single up 103
Sleeping 16, 140
Slip 102–105
Spinnakers 86–90
– dangers 88
– drop 89–90
– the gybe 89
– hoisting 88–89
Spring off 105
Square knot 29
Stanchion 8
Starboard 8
Starboard tack 46
Steering 38–43
– astern 40–41
– under engine 38–41
– under sail 54–64
Stern 8
Stern line 19, 97, 108, 115

Stern spring 19, 97, 108, 115
Stop button/lever 37
Storm jib 80
Sweat 106
Swinging mooring 119–126

Tack 48–50, 65, 74
Tailing 23
Telltales 44–45, 95
Tender 134–135
Tides 165
Throttle and gear control 35
Throwing line 153
Tiller 8, 38
Toe rail 8
Toilet 12–13
Topping lift 18, 65
Topsides 8
Transom 8
Traveller 94
Trim 44–45
– advanced trimming 92–95

Up to wind 47
Uphaul 18, 87

Vang 65
VHF radio 153, 161–162

Warp 8, 19, 97
Wash board 8
Watch 136–137, 140
Water maker 11
Weather 165
Weather helm 54–55
Wheel 8, 38
Winch 8, 22–25
– barrel 22
– handle 8, 22, 23

Yacht skippering 162–168
– theory knowledge 164–165
– practical skills 166–167
– technical skills 167
– under sail 54–64